DRIVE HENRY VIII AND ANNE BOLEYN'S ROYAL ROAD TRIP

FOLLOW IN THE FOOTSTEPS OF THE 1535 ROYAL PROGRESS OF ENGLAND

MICROCAMPER CAPERS

DREAM ROADTRIPS AT YOUR FINGERTIPS

THE ROYAL ROUTE SERIES

AN OVERVIEW TO TUDOR ENGLAND

In 1485, Henry VII's victory over Richard III at the Battle of Bosworth ended the brutal Wars of the Roses. He strengthened his position by limiting aristocratic power and kept the peace while amassing a solid financial foundation, often at the expense of his subjects.

The extravagant Henry VIII, tall, handsome, and cultured, was a stark contrast to his austere father. During his reign, art and commerce flourished. Many people benefited from the cloth trade, but peasants suffered as more and more land was converted to pasture.

Henry's reign was overshadowed by his need for a legitimate male heir. In twenty years, Catherine of Aragon first bore him a daughter but no sons. Desperate, Henry attempted to marry Anne Boleyn, finally succeeding in 1533, when he declared that he, not the Pope, was the head of the English Church. His decision triggered the Reformation, the most significant event of the Tudor period, shaping the course of English history for centuries to come.

Henry launched the Dissolution of the Monasteries with his minister Thomas Cromwell investigating abbeys on the 1535 progress. Protests and revolts were brutally suppressed. The confiscated monastic wealth bolstered the king's coffers and many of his favoured subjects.

A suspicious and increasingly tyrannical Henry still sought to secure the Tudor dynasty. Anne gave him a daughter, Elizabeth but no sons. Anne was executed.

Jane Seymour died with the longed-for boy, Edward, in her arms. Then, shortly after, Anne of Cleves was rejected. His next wife, Katherine Howard, was beheaded for treason and adultery. Katherine Parr, Henry's final wife, helped his daughters, Mary and Elizabeth become queens.

Elizabeth I was one of England's most astute and successful monarchs. She resisted marriage proposals and worked hard to maintain her image as Gloriana, a Virgin Queen wedded not to a man but to an increasingly prosperous England. Throughout the 16th century, most people's quality of life steadily improved. However, this was not the case for everyone, and late in Elizabeth's reign, a series of Poor Laws addressed the long-standing issue of begging.

Elizabeth, however, was not universally adored. Although her establishment of a moderately Protestant Church of England satisfied many of her subjects, it alienated Catholics even more, prompting plots to replace her with her cousin Mary, Queen of Scots.

Elizabeth's execution of Mary in 1587 accelerated a clash with Spain. England had long contested Spain in the New World, where Francis Drake and other explorers forged new trade routes. In 1588, Philip II sent his Armada against England, but it was defeated by a combination of English seamanship, fireships, good fortune, and bad weather.

Dying childless, the crown went to King James VI of Scotland, a decedent of Henry VII, and the Stuart dynasty began.

CONTENTS

Route overview 4
How to use this guide 6
The 1535 progress route 7
Who was King Henry VIII? 8
Tudor royal progresses 10
Daily life in Henry's England 13
How Anne Boleyn became queen 19
Henry and Anne In 1535 22
Tudor travel 23
Hunting with hawks 27
Start: Windsor 30
1. Reading 34
2. Ewelme Palace 38
3. Abingdon 41
4. King John's Palace Langley 44
5. Sudeley Castle 47
6. Tewkesbury 51
7. Gloucester 53
8. Gloucestershire environs 56
9. Leonard Stanley 59
10. Berkeley Castle 61
11. Thornbury 64
12. Iron Acton 66
13. Little Sodbury 69
14. Bromham 72
15. Burbage 74
16. Thruxton 76
17. Hurstbourne Priors 80
18. Winchester 83
19. Bishop's Waltham 86
20. Southampton 88
21. Portchester 91
22. Salisbury 94
23. Clarendon Palace 97
24. Sherbourne St John 99
25. Old Basing 101
26. Bramshill 104
27. Easthamstead 106
The arrests in May 1536 108
The ones that 'got away' 114
The trials begin 117
The trials continue 119
Examining the trials 121
The executions begin 126
The remainder of the reign 130
Tudor food 137
Make a Tudor recipe 139
Packing list 140
Phone apps and websites 144
Handy tips for microcamping 146
Road trip games 150
Places to eat 151
Campsites 159
Further reading 163
Index 164

3

ROUTE OVERVIEW

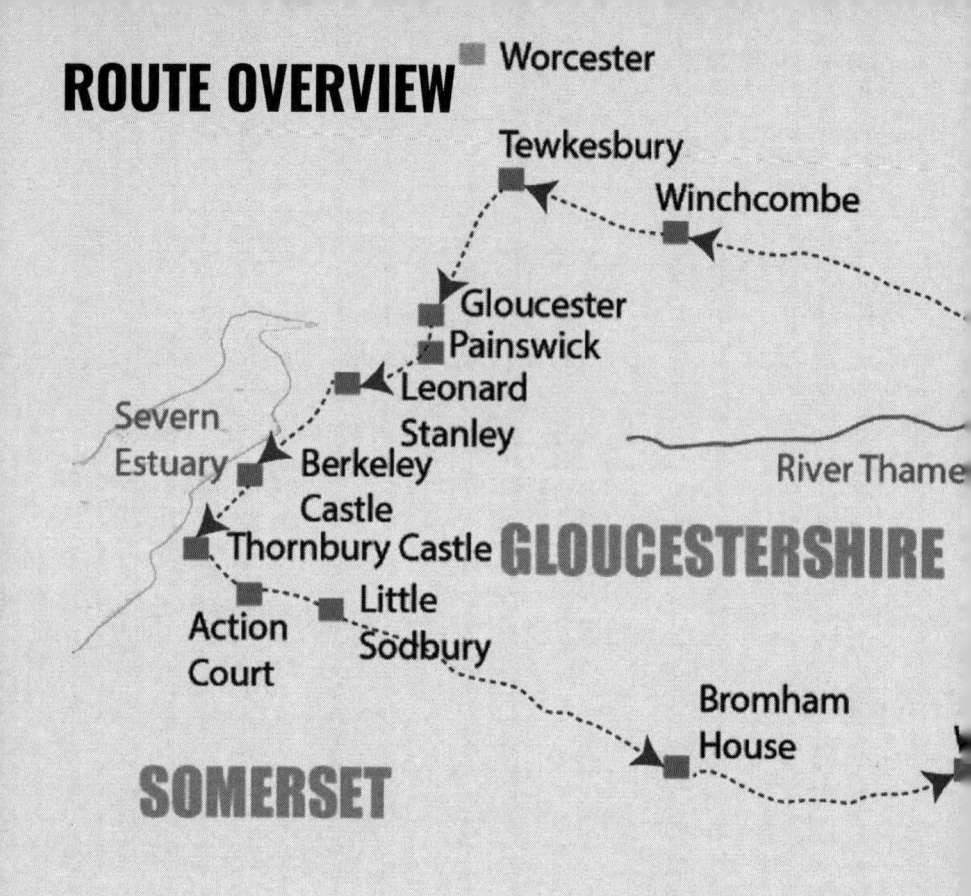

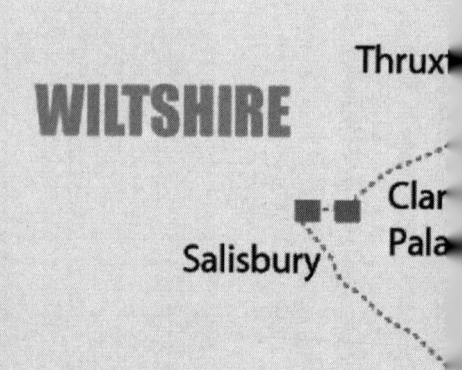

N ↑

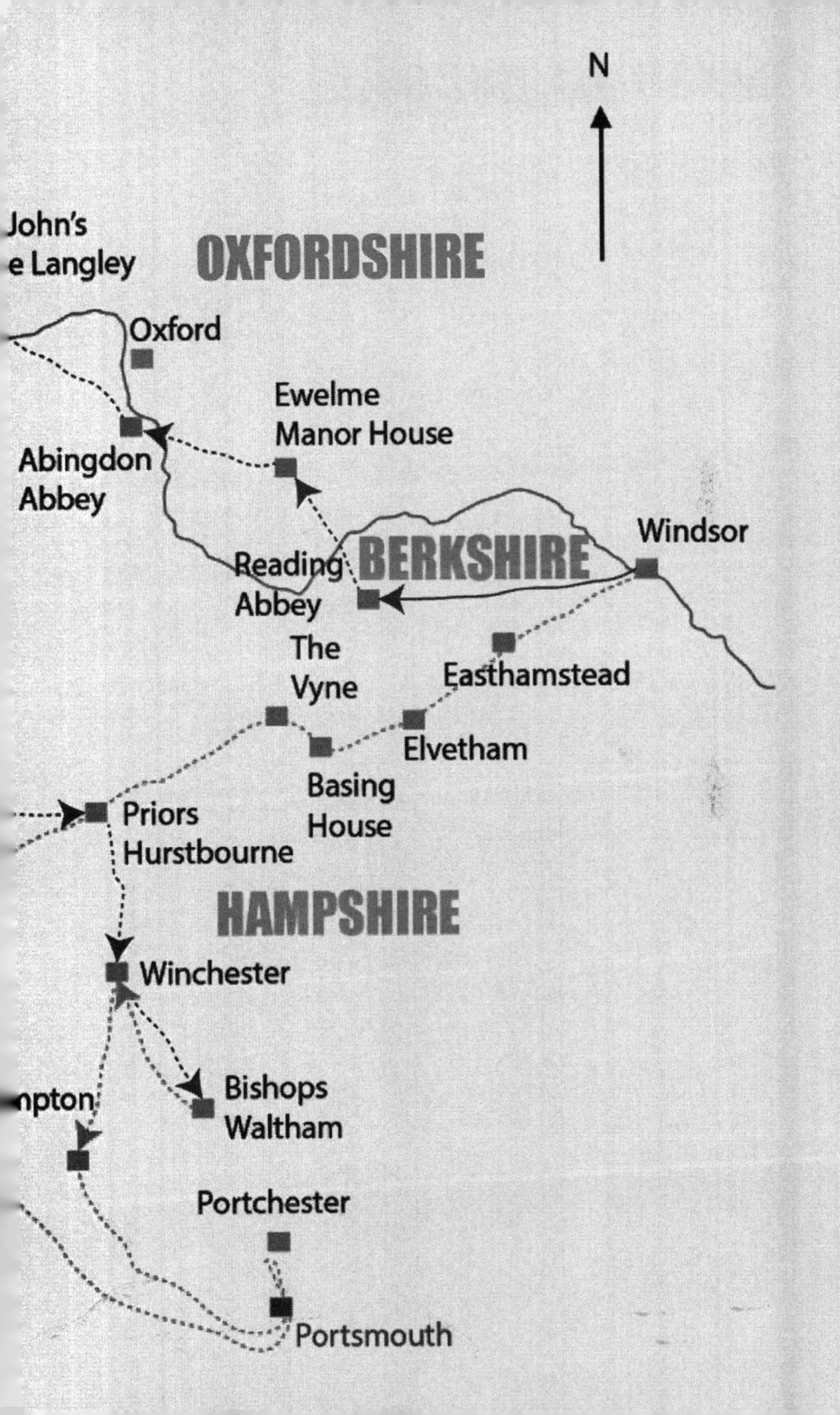

OXFORDSHIRE

John's
e Langley

Oxford

Ewelme
Manor House

Abingdon
Abbey

BERKSHIRE

Reading
Abbey

Windsor

The
Vyne

Easthamstead

Elvetham

Basing
House

Priors
Hurstbourne

HAMPSHIRE

Winchester

Bishops
Waltham

mpton

Portchester

Portsmouth

HOW TO USE THIS GUIDE

1. Plan where you want to start on the circular route
2. Use the postcodes to plan your journey
3. Visit stops that still stand
4. Decide which ruined sites you want to see (if any)
5. Pick extra points of interest near the stops if you have time
6. Check out the list of eateries for refreshments
7. Use the list to plan your campsites or stealth camp

TIP: Use Google Maps to find things nearby, e.g., Find tea rooms near [Postcode] or Find tea rooms along route [Place] to [Place]

See the full route on Google Maps: https://rebrand.ly/1535Map

REMEMBER

Sat navs can take you on inappropriate routes that might not be suitable for your vehicle (or your constitution!) If it's getting tricky, stop and replan.

Check the websites for places you plan to visit for opening times, prices and further information to avoid disappointment. Many on this route are not open all year round, and some are ruins. There are suggestions for alternative attractions at these sites.

THE 1535 PROGRESS ROUTE

In the summer of 1535, the king took his progress westward, planning to travel from Windsor to Bristol and back in a large circular route, staying at one of his 60-plus royal properties in the south, or with noblemen, courtiers, or monastic houses. Stays at Reading, Abingdon and Tewkesbury Abbeys were on the cards for that year. Henry planned to visit his towns and cities. He would hear the complaints of the poor. And there would be fun. The king and queen would ride and hunt liberally. Leading religious reformers and loyal movers and shakers at court would be schmoozed with at their country piles and bestowed with honours. Onside-bishops would be invested to help establish the new Church of England, with Henry its supreme head.

The months following the progress had a dramatic effect on the nation, the king, and most of all Anne, who would be left holding her linen cap away from her neck, to make the swordsman's job easier.

This guidebook brings the summer of 1535 back to life and gives you a chance to ponder what changed for Henry and Anne along the way and the array of people caught up in their very public marital breakdown.

There will also be some lighter moments describing what daily life was like for someone in Tudor times, from a falconer training Henry's hunting hawks to a tired commoner travelling along badly rutted roads to a welcoming coaching inn.

In the words of Henry:

'Of all losses, time is the most irrecuperable for it can never be redeemed.'

So, let's get going!

WHO WAS KING HENRY VIII?

Overview

Henry was born on 28 June 1491 and reigned from 22 April 1509 until his death nearly 55 years later, on 28 January 1547. Contemporaries saw young Henry as an attractive, educated, and accomplished king. He was a writer and composer, described as *'one of the most charismatic rulers to sit on the English throne'*. Dangerously overweight as he grew older, suffering from sporting injuries and painful ulceration of the legs from which he got little respite, his health and temper suffered as a result. He is typically portrayed as a lusty, arrogant, paranoid, and increasingly despotic monarch in his later years. Does he deserve that?

Henry is primarily known for his six marriages, notably his struggle to have his first marriage to Catherine of Aragon annulled. His quarrel with Pope Clement VII over it prompted Henry to launch the English Reformation, which liberated the Church of England from papal authority. He proclaimed himself Supreme Head of the Church of England and dismantled convents and monasteries, for which he was excommunicated.

But it wasn't all acrimony and disaster. Henry is also recognised as the *'the father of the Royal Navy'* since he invested substantially in maritime defence, expanding its strength from a handful to more than 50 warships and establishing the Navy Board. In addition, he built naval dockyards on the Thames and in Portsmouth, which he would visit on the 1535 progress.

Domestically, Henry is remembered for making dramatic reforms to the English constitution, ushering in the notion of the divine right of monarchs. During his reign, he also significantly increased royal power. He routinely used charges of treason and heresy to stifle dissent, and individuals charged were frequently executed without a formal trial using Bills of Attainder.

Many of his political goals were accomplished through the efforts of his chief ministers, some of whom were exiled or executed when they fell out of his favour. Thomas Wolsey, Thomas More, Thomas Cromwell, Sir Richard Rich, and Thomas Cranmer all played essential roles in his administration. However, only Wolsey and Rich would avoid a Tudor execution.

Henry was a lavish spender, utilising the revenues from the dissolution of the monasteries as well as acts of the Reformation Parliament. He also changed the rules, so the money that was formerly paid to Rome became royal revenue. Despite the money from these sources, he was constantly on the verge of financial ruin due to his personal extravagance and his numerous costly and largely unsuccessful wars, particularly with King Francis I of France, Holy Roman Emperor Charles V, and King James V of Scotland.

His domestic policy meant he oversaw the legal unification of England and Wales, and he was the first English monarch to rule as King of Ireland with the Crown of Ireland Act 1542.

The need for a son

Henry life was dominated and determined by his desire to have sons. He and his contemporaries believed that one of his most essential duties as king was to provide at least one adult male heir to succeed him peacefully when he died.

This was not because Henry was simply misogynistic. Instead, there was no precedence for female rule. England had never had a crowned 'queen regnant', which means a ruling queen, instead of a king's partner and 'queen consort'.

In the twelfth century, Matilda, Henry I's daughter, ascended to the throne and was soon challenged by her cousin, Stephen of Blois. It sparked a civil war. Matilda was never crowned.

Henry was equally concerned that if one of his daughters succeeded him, it would spark civil war or, worse, she would marry a foreign prince, bringing England under the control of a foreign power or dynasty, as it did when Mary married Philip II of Spain.

This all meant Henry needed a son. He also required that his son be at least fifteen years old when he died. Younger children could not reign independently and would be governed by a regent or council of councillors. As Richard III and the murder of the 'Princes in the Tower' had demonstrated, regents were not always to be trusted. Even if the young monarch survived, if there were several counsellors, their power struggle would imperil the country's peace and security.

Educated by the harsh realities of medieval life, Henry had grown up knowing his history. He understood that England had been in a state of bloody civil war for thirty years before his father became king. Only the usurping of the throne by killing a king in battle and the marriage of his Lancastrian father and Yorkist mother had brought peace to England. Henry VIII did not wish to return his realm to bloodshed.

The best insurance policy would be a line of adult princes. This meant acting quickly. Henry was just seventeen years old when his father died at the age of fifty-two. While it might look like he had plenty of life left in him, he was concerned that he might die in his fifties without a strong male successor if he did not have a son by his early thirties. Unfortunately, that is exactly what happened. His young son Edward inherited the throne was just nine years old. Children perished quickly. The boy was dead six years later, his poor lungs ruined by tuberculosis—although that didn't stop some contemporaries suspecting poisoning. Henry's own younger brother, Arthur, had died when he was fifteen. Henry's illegitimate son, Henry Fitzroy, died at seventeen.

Tudor England's peace and prosperity depended on the fruit of his wife, then wives' wombs.

TUDOR ROYAL PROGRESSES

The king listening to a religious reformer

Why go on a progress?

For four reasons, Tudor monarchs rarely stayed in one place for long periods, particularly during the summer.

Firstly, wealthy people relocated to avoid seasonal outbreaks of plague or a mysterious disease called *'sweating sickness'* in London.

Secondly, due to the size and scale of the procession, they ate so much food that a host's or even a small town's resources were quickly depleted. Meanwhile, the waste accumulated, causing problems for the locals.

Thirdly, the progress was an important event for observers as well as the monarch. They served a vital political function for the establishment in an era before mass communication by allowing local gentry and officials to access and show loyalty to their sovereign. Honours could be given to those people who helped the king achieve his objectives.

Finally, progresses were popular with the wider population too. They allowed the monarch to be seen all over the country. This reinforced the monarchy's authority and presence within the realm.

Forming a procession of a mile or more, the court moved around the country, staying at a string of royal residences, noble houses, and monasteries along a predetermined itinerary called a *'geist'*, which was published in June.

The much-anticipated list defined each Tudor progress. It specified where and how long the king planned to stay. It also kept track of how far he would travel between stops. The mileage would vary. In the summer of 1535, the court usually travelled between six and 14 miles per day, but it could be as much as 20 or more if logistics demanded it. In 1528, the average was nine miles daily. Depending on the terrain, the court travelled by horseback most of the time, but river or sea travel would also be used on occasion.

At the start of the Tudor dynasty, progresses were a form of *'spin'* for him. Relationship management was vital for Henry VII because he ascended to the throne following the infamous Battle of Bosworth, slaying Plantagenet King Richard III. At the start of his reign, the country was still in turmoil. Not everyone was *'pleased'* with their new *'ruler'*. Different factions were still vying for the throne, all thinking *'their man'* had a legitimate claim to the crown.

To help quell rebellion, Henry VII took these long journeys around his new kingdom, travelling to towns and cities to listen to people's complaints and trying to appease them. He declared himself the *'true king'*, keen to *'get things done'* for the nation and demonstrated that his dynasty was here to stay.

Young Prince Hal toured the country with his father for the same peacekeeping and political purposes, although when it was Henry's turn to rule his reign in 1509, it was on a firmer footing, thanks to Henry VII clinging on to power for 24 years.

For the new king, the purely *'authority-strengthening'* aspect to progresses was not as important. This meant there was some free time for pursuing pleasure rather than just pen-pushing politics. And while hunting was a fun pastime for Henry, it was also a method for ambitious courtiers and dignitaries to gain the king's attention. Access to their prime hunting grounds was a real draw for the sovereign. (You will see some of them as you drive the route.)

and children and their households accompanied him. Regardless of how complicated the logistics of moving 750 to 1,500 people might be, Henry recognised the importance of getting out among his citizens and allowing his subjects to see him in the flesh from the start of his reign. And what a sight it must have been, the king and queen on horseback, resplendent in their riding garb, flanked by their vast and impressive retinue. (See the Gloucester entry for an example of this.)

A reenactor's tent and cooking pots

Hundreds of carriages and carts would rumble through the countryside, carrying everything from clothes to tents, hunting gear to jewellery, chests bursting at the seams with coins, the king's bed, and probably a kitchen sink or two.

A sea of tents, forming a patchwork of all colours and sizes, would materialise as mallets whacked tent pegs into the ground. Hundreds of campfires would fill the air with smoke that wafted

Who else went on the progress?

The headcount varied greatly depending on whether the king's wife across the site. Hot food simmered in gigantic pans. Dogs barked, crowds whistled, shouted, and hooted. There would be calls to deliver refreshment, and many a beer cask would be cracked open. As the night wore on, more travellers would attach themselves to the camp's perimeter like barnacles to a boat.

HOW WAS A ROUTE DECIDED?

Tudor progresses were usually planned during the '*grass season*,' which was between August and October when the hay was being cut, other agricultural work was minimal, the weather was ideal for hunting, and the daylight hours were long.

Hosting the monarch and their court was a great honour and a clear sign of royal favour. However, it also came at a significant financial outlay, with grand festivities and large banquets to honour the king and queen, plus housing them and the closest in their entourage. In Gloucestershire, you will see Acton Court, Nicholas Poyntz not only redecorated the royal apartments but he also built an entirely new wing of his house in preparation for Henry and Anne's visit.

The length of Henry's stay was determined by several factors, including the residence's size, suitability, and level of luxury, plus the proximity of good hunting grounds, of course. A visit could last anywhere from a few hours to a month! Longer stays were reserved for larger ecclesiastical palaces, religious houses, or royal properties.

A modern banquet

Visiting prestigious places meant the king and his royal guests were always welcomed with great pomp and ceremony, regardless of whether the host was an abbot, nobleman, courtier, or a place.

In towns, the mayor and other dignitaries would meet the royal party at the outskirts, where the two processions would merge and ride in formation to the cathedral or main church. Pageants were sometimes included in the reception but were usually reserved for international guests, such as when Charles V, Holy Roman Emperor and King of Spain, entered London in 1522.

Following that, the royal party would make an offering at the church before being escorted to their lodgings, where gifts would be exchanged. (See the stop descriptions later, which bring to life Henry's arrival in town.)

Sometimes a geist would need to be adapted due to changes in the weather, food shortages, and disease outbreaks. 1535 was no different. Henry and

Anne planned to travel through the West Country to Bristol before returning to Windsor, but they were forced to abandon their plans due to the plague besieging the city. Instead, they stayed at nearby Thornbury Castle, where a delegation of Bristol residents travelled out to pay their respects and give the royal couple gifts. In Hampshire, they also deviated, avoiding Old Alresford, Alton, and Farnham for the same reason.

On rare occasions, the whim of the king would mean further changes. In 1535, the royal couple were so taken with the hunting in Hampshire that they delayed their return to Windsor by nearly a month. New geists had to be hurriedly planned for the *'merrie'* hawking couple. This was no insignificant task. Not only were there hundreds of people to move, but the monarchs also brought a lot of possessions with them—all those plates, beds, tapestries, and large chests of coins and clothing.

The task of packing, transporting, and furnishing the royal lodgings at each destination was handled by special servants. Before the royal couple arrived, the Clerk of the Market and other court officers would ride ahead to ensure enough room for the entire party. Before the king arrived, they would warn the *'people to bake, brew, and make ready other food and drink in their lodgings.'* The Officers of the Wardrobe would pack and transport the goods by cart, mule or boat and the Grooms of the Chamber were responsible for setting up and furnishing the royal lodgings at each new destination.

Tudor furniture

DAILY LIFE IN HENRY'S ENGLAND

The royal court

At the top of the tree was the king, of course, followed by the court. So, who was a courtier, and what did they do?

The court was a group of people who accompanied the king wherever he went in the hopes of fulfilling his wishes in exchange for money, land, or favours.

Bucking the trend, Henry's court had *'tweaked'* existing structure to suit his own ends.

Chief minister: an unofficial position. The chief minister was the most powerful person in the government, reporting directly to the king. Henry liked to fill this role with someone who delighted in details and paperwork—because he didn't.

Thomas Cromwell

Previously, the chief minister was a high ranking nobleman. Henry changed that. At the time of the 1535 progress, the role was taken on by the son of a Putney blacksmith who had rocketed to power with his legal prowess, Thomas Cromwell (he of Wolf Hall on the BBC) who was the *'chief enforcer'* of Henry's will. Before Thomas was another Thomas, the son of a prosperous Ipswich merchant, Cardinal Thomas Wolsey until he died travelling back to London from York for his trial (where things were not expected to end well.) More on this later.

Why do this if it wasn't the way *'things were done'* at court up to that point?

Henry liked to appoint *'lesser'* people to prominent positions as they owed him far more loyalty than one of the elite. The blue-blooded aristocracy expected titles to be lavished on them. If their family members secured enough prominent positions, there was always the risk the household would try to usurp Henry. The nobility was incensed that their power and influence was being given to these *'undeservings'*. Things hadn't been like that before, and the aristocracy's fury tended to boil over.

(You'll meet a lot of these ambitious nobles and the next group as you learn more about the personalities found at the stops.)

Privy chamber: members were allowed to enter the king's private quarters and had special access to him. One of them, the Guard of the Stool, looked after the king as he used the toilet (or *'closed stool'*). Modern-day Blackadder actor Sir Tony Robinson listed this as one of his *'worst jobs in history'*. Nevertheless, in Tudor times, roles like those, along with sleeping on the hard floor while the king snoozed in his plush bed, were highly prized.

Why? Because they gained access to the king's ear, and often these men became close friends of the monarch. (Many of the winners and losers on the progress will be in this group.)

Royal household: servants and officials who looked after the king's affairs and the royal court. This didn't mean managing putting the royal bins out. On the contrary, the high ranking roles gave considerable power.

Royal council: These were men chosen by the king to provide advice, but he didn't have to accept what they said, and often, towards the end of his reign, he didn't. Expensive foreign wars and aggressive religious reform that was rankling the traditionalists at court, plus abbots, priors, monks and nuns and the wider population, were two such examples.

Beneath these upper echelons of society were plenty more levels before the common man or woman, beyond thankful to get a bumper-sized turnip in a harvest, would appear.

The wider population

When Henry Tudor seized the throne in 1485, England had a population of less than two million people. Perhaps another half-million people lived in Wales. Scotland and Ireland's figures are speculative at best.

By the time his granddaughter Elizabeth I died in 1603, England and Wales had grown to a population of over four million people. Rural areas were home to more than 90% of the population. At the outset of the era, London had a population of only 50,000 people. By the end, it had quadrupled in size to 200,000 people. At any given period, the capital housed roughly half of all city dwellers. This small but dynamic population would grow into a cultural force whose ideas and way of life would shape not only the future of Britain but the entire world.

The rural majority was still socially organised based on land ownership. The aristocracy at the top of the tree—confined to those with titles as peers of the realm—owned many vast estates, ran households of up to 150 people, and commuted between their estates and a London townhouse on a regular basis. Their political and power lives were quite public.

The gentry, whose land holdings were often smaller and more concentrated geographically, sat underneath them. Officially, a gentleman was someone who had the right to a coat of arms, but in practice, a gentleman was someone who lived according to generally accepted standards, such as not working, owning, and renting out land for others to work on, maintaining a suitable-sized house, dressing appropriately, and entertaining on a suitable scale. Gentlemen wore the best woollen broadcloths adorned with silks and furs, sat down to three or four meat dishes at dinner, and were expected to lead local society and occupy public office. (These people did very well when Thomas Cromwell redistributed the lands and assets liquidated during the Dissolution of the Monasteries.)

The yeomen were far more numerous. Their land was frequently rented from those above them, while many of them also owned pieces of it and farmed it all themselves. Some of the gentlemen were wealthier than others in terms of pure riches, but theirs was a life of active involvement on the land. Most of their servants were farm hands who helped till the soil and care for livestock, rather than personal or domestic helpers. Some held minor government jobs, such as churchwarden or constable, but they were primarily wealthy farmers with four- or five-room homes, good wool clothing, and bellies filled with modest but hearty dinners.

The husbandmen followed. They farmed their rented lands on a much lesser scale. Their residences were typically two-room affairs, and much of the labour was done alone by family members. They were the most numerous of all the groups that ranked about the labourers. They had few amenities or luxuries in their life.

Below the husbandmen were the labourers, who had no land of their own and had to hire themselves out for a daily pay to their socially superior neighbours. It was a precarious existence, with most people living in single-room hovels and eating bread and little else.

A re-enactor blacksmithing

What about the urban population?

International merchants occupying the top posts, serving as mayors, living in huge, well-furnished, and well-staffed town residences, occasionally hobnobbing with the landed aristocracy, formed the minority of England's modest urban populace.

National merchants were the next step down, hiring apprentices as legalised slaves and enjoying a slightly more comfortable existence than yeomen, but on a comparable social level.

Craftsmen, helped by their apprentices and family, occupied the next slot, which usually included a home one or two rooms in addition to a workshop.

And, just like in the countryside, the bottom of the pile was day labourers.

Food costs account for roughly 17% of total income in the United Kingdom in modern times. Food accounted for around 80% of most people's expenses during the Tudor period.

To grasp what money meant to a craftsman considering a new coat, it's important to consider their disposable income or what was left over after the family had been fed and the rent had been paid. A husbandman's wife had to weigh one set of monetary needs against another when deciding whether to buy ale, make it herself, or let the family make do with water.

A skilled man could command a wage of 4d a day when he was working at the start of the Tudor period, and women could earn about half that. A skilled wage had risen to around 6d by the end of the era. These figures represented the absolute minimum level of survival for a small family working full-time.

There was enough to sustain a simple, low-cost diet, but not much more.

Tudor advancement... and downfall...

Cardinal Thomas Wolsey

Social hierarchy was relatively rigid in Tudor times. Nonetheless, a surprising amount of social mobility was still possible. As you saw with Henry's choices of chief minister, miracles did happen, although the meteoric rise was often not permanent. There were three options for those seeking social advancement: the church, the law, and service.

Despite being the lowly son of an Ipswich butcher and cattle farmer, Thomas Wolsey became Henry's closest and most trusted adviser through his position as cardinal. The cardinal's administrative ability was admired by Henry, who disliked drowning in paperwork (*understandable!*) was happy to delegate it to his right-hand man. As a result, he became Henry's Lord Chancellor, the highest of the Great Officers of State.

Despite being born a mere gentleman, Thomas Cranmer owed his position as Archbishop of Canterbury to the church and would later remind Bishop of Winchester, Stephen Gardiner, '*I pray God that we, being called to the name of lords, have not forgotten our own baser estates, that once we were simple esquires.*' Cranmer was appointed the resident ambassador at the court of the Holy Roman Emperor, Charles V, in January 1532. While Cranmer was following Charles through Italy, he received a royal letter dated 1 October 1532. He had been appointed the new Archbishop of Canterbury following the death of the previous incumbent, Bishop William Warham and was ordered to return to England PDQ.

The appointment to the most high-ranking clerical post in the land had been secured by the Boleyns. It caused great surprise amongst the religious fraternity as Cranmer had previously held only minor positions in the church thus far.

Thomas More

Like Cromwell, Sir Thomas More's training as a lawyer aided his rise to prominence, although his great mind was not enough to save him. He was executed 3 days before the 1635 progress set off from Windsor for high treason. He could not reconcile himself with the king's plans for himself, Anne, and the church.

The life of Sir John Thynne demonstrated the value of service in noble households as a means of bettering oneself. His position as steward to Jane Seymour's elder brother Edward, the Duke of Somerset, enabled him to amass enough wealth to build a large and showy *'prodigy house'* in Wiltshire. All these centuries later, you might know it? *'Longleat.'*

Famously, Putney-born son of a blacksmith, Thomas Cromwell, later Earl of Essex, became Henry's right-hand man after the death of Wolsey. Thomas would take part in the progress, eyeing up monasteries to dissolve as he went. His enemies would see Cromwell get his comeuppance for arranging Henry's disastrous marital match with Anne of Cleves, amongst other *'misdemeanours'* they felt he had committed.

Henry's reliance on commoners created a period of frustration for many of the great blue-blooded nobles, including men like Edward Stafford, Duke of Buckingham and Thomas Howard, Duke of Norfolk, who did not feel they were receiving the level of honour and share of power that their forefathers had.

Buckingham was one of few peers with substantial Plantagenet blood in his veins. His activities with his extended family attracted suspicion. Nine years into Henry's reign, in 1520, Buckingham was suspected of treason, and the king authorised an investigation, even personally examining witnesses against him.

Enough evidence was gathered for a trial. The duke was finally summoned to court in April 1521, arrested and placed in the tower. He was tried before a panel of 17 peers, being accused of listening to prophecies of the king's death and intending to kill him. Buckingham was executed on Tower Hill on 17 May that year. There was no escaping Henry's wrath even after death. Buckingham was posthumously attained by Act of Parliament on 31 July 1523, disinheriting most of his wealth from his children. That was how Ewelme, visited by Anne and Henry on 12 July 1535, became a crown property.

In Tudor England, there were correct and incorrect ways to advance oneself.

Henry had grown up knowing his history: he knew that England had been in a state of bloody civil war for thirty years before his father became king, fought between the Lancastrians and the Yorkists (the Wars of the Roses). The marriage of his parents, him a Lancastrian, her a Yorkist, had brought peace to England, and Henry didn't want to return it to bloodshed.

To keep it from happening again, he needed a line of adult princes. This meant acting quickly: Henry was only seventeen years old when his father died at fifty-two. He was concerned that he would die in his fifties without an adult, independent male heir if he did not have a son by his early thirties.

As you follow in the footsteps of Henry and Anne, you will discover the stories of many of the winners and losers of the Tudor period. Despite wanting to avoid bloodshed, it is estimated around 57,000 people were executed during his reign. So perhaps you'll want to be on your best behaviour during your progress, just to be on the safe side?

HOW ANNE BOLEYN BECAME QUEEN

Anne's rise

Anne Boleyn

The king's love for Anne Boleyn appears to have begun around 1526. An ardent letter from him survives, most likely written in 1527, which declares he had been *'for more than a year now struck by the dart of love.'* He begged her to *'give yourself body and heart to me'* and become his *'sole mistress.'* Not wanting to be a mere *'mistress'* like her sister and many others, Anne refused his kind offer, and the couple had agreed to marry by the summer of 1527. Unfortunately, it would take another five years for that to happen.

Many of Henry's love letters penned to Anne in the late 1520s were preserved by chance in the Vatican Library. The couple had been separated by illness when Anne retired to the family home of Hever Castle after becoming ill with *'sweating sickness,'* a virulent and often fatal disease. Henry needed to avoid it at all costs since he still lacked a male heir after almost 20 years of marriage.

One of these passionate letters, originally written in French, can still be seen in translation at Hever. Anne's signature can be found on two *'Books of Hours'*, beautiful, illuminated personal prayer books. Is her inscription: *'Le temps viendra / Je Anne Boleyn'* (*'The time will come / I Anne Boleyn'*) a reference to the period of longing and waiting during which Wolsey tried to wrangle with the pope—freeing Henry from his marriage to Catherine of Aragon so that he could marry her. Catherine of Aragon's fall

According to reports, the pope refused to listen to Henry's detailed liturgical appeals that it was *'forbidden for a man to marry his brother's wife'*.

Earlier, Catherine had been married to Henry's older brother, Arthur, Prince of Wales. She was only three when she was betrothed to the heir apparent of the English throne. The daughter of Isabella I of Castile and Ferdinand II of Aragon, in 1501, they married, but Arthur died suddenly five months later at Ludlow Castle, 40 miles northwest of Gloucester.

As time went on, a skilled stateswoman, Catherine was the first known female ambassador in European history, serving as the Aragonese ambassador to England in 1507. In 1509, she married the newly ascended Henry. Things were going well. Quite revelatory for the time, the new king trusted a woman to rule for six months in 1513, while he was in France, fighting in the Battle of Spurs

Alas, the all-important male heirs eluded the couple. Only a girl, Mary, survived into adulthood. Henry was frustrated, and after his roving eye had scanned quite a few ladies of the court, it settled on the vivacious Anne.

Although Henry had been married for over a decade, the question of the marriage's validity burned bright in Henry's mind. Annulling the marriage to Catherine meant that his one child, daughter Princess Mary, was illegitimate. Still, he claimed that Catherine's inability to bear children was a clear sign of God's displeasure, and everything would go swimmingly with a new, *'more appropriate'*, wife.

Henry hoped the new pope, Clement VII, would take the easy route, admit his predecessor's error, and quickly annul the marriage. Now in his thirties, Henry's biological clock ticked loudly. Henry's all-consuming quest for an annulment became known colloquially as the *'King's Great Matter.'* Great minds scoured the bible for those all-important liturgical reasons for Henry to become footloose and fancy-free again.

Anne saw Henry's infatuation and the moral quandary as a convenient opportunity to advance herself. She resolved to accept his embrace only as his *'acknowledged queen'*. She began to share his place in policy and in state, but not yet in his bed.

In 1527, the king's secretary, William Knight, was sent to Pope Clement to seek the annulment on the grounds that Julius II's dispensing bull allowing him to marry his brother's widow had been obtained fraudulently. The answer was a firm, *'no!'*

The following year, sweating sickness erupted with ferocity. The mortality rate in London was sky-high. The terrified court dispersed throughout the land. Henry left London, changing residence frequently. Anne retreated to the safety of the family home, Hever Castle, 30 miles from London, but still contracted the illness. Her brother-in-law died from it. Henry dispatched his own physician to Hever to care for Anne, and she recovered quickly.

Princess Mary, later Mary I

Keen to be free of Catherine, Henry pinned his hopes on a direct appeal to Rome, acting independently of Wolsey. He had revealed nothing about his plans for Anne to his chief minister.

Knight had trouble gaining access to the pope because Clement was a prisoner of Emperor Charles V, Catherine's nephew. He was forced to return with a conditional dispensation, which Wolsey insisted was insufficient. Henry had no choice but to entrust his *'Great Matter'* to Wolsey, who did everything he could to secure a decision in Henry's favour, even going so far as to convene an ecclesiastical court in England, with a special emissary from Pope Clement, Lorenzo Campeggio, to decide the matter.

Clement might have sent Campeggio to attend, but he had not delegated decision-making authority to him. The outward *'ticking of the box'* was a trick. Charles V was devoted to his aunt and acted in her interests, rather than Clement's or Henry's. Thus, Henry was forbidden from marrying until an official decision was made in Rome—not England.

Convinced that Wolsey's allegiances were firmly with the pope, not England, Anne, along with Wolsey's many enemies, attempted his removal from office in 1529. Finally, Henry agreed to Wolsey's arrest, and he might have been executed for treason if he hadn't died of illness in 1530 on his way back from York. Catherine was expelled from court in 1531, two years before Henry married Anne. Her rooms were given to his new love.

Catherine's supporters were unwavering. In the autumn of 1531, Anne was dining at a manor on the Thames. An enraged mob of women arrived, forcing Anne to flee by boat.

Thomas Cranmer

After seven years of delay and much wrangling with the papacy, numerous Acts of Parliament finally authorised the break with Rome. The newly appointed Archbishop of Canterbury, Thomas Cranmer, swiftly annulled Henry's marriage to Catherine on May 23, 1533.

By this point, a forty-plus Henry, keen to move on, had already married Anne twice, once secretly in Dover in November 1532 and again privately but officially in January 1533.

Anne was crowned queen consort on 1 June 1533 in a magnificent ceremony at Westminster Abbey, followed by a lavish banquet. She was England's first queen consort to be crowned with St Edward's Crown, previously only used to crown monarchs, and the last to be crowned separately from her husband. Anne's pregnancy was visible at the time, and the child was assumed to be male. The day before, Anne had taken part in an elaborate procession through the streets of London, seated in a carriage of *'white cloth of gold'* that rested on two Palfrey horses clothed to the ground in white damask. The Cinque Ports barons of Hastings, New Romney, Hythe, Dover, Sandwich, and Rye, held a canopy of gold cloth above her head. She was dressed in white, wearing a delicate gold coronet on her head, her long dark hair tumbled down freely beneath it.

Henry hoped Anne and the child she carried would provide the much needed male heir, but again, the couple had a daughter, Elizabeth, born a few weeks prematurely on 7 September 1533, between three and four o'clock in the afternoon. The girl's birth came as a shock to her parents, who had hoped for a boy. All the royal physicians and astrologers, except one, had predicted a son. The French king had been asked to serve as the prince's godfather. The prepared letters announcing the birth of a *'prince'* were now hastily amended to read *'princess'*. The traditional jousting tournament celebrating the birth of an heir was cancelled. Sadly, all Anne's subsequent male children were miscarried

HENRY AND ANNE IN 1535

Events during and shortly after the summer progress would shape Henry and Anne's futures—fatally for her. The queen fell pregnant again on the tour with the soon to be cherished male heir. In January 1536, Henry had his near-fatal jousting accident, which undermined his mental and physical health. It was said the shock caused Anne to miscarry.

Some said she was a witch and had given birth to a deformed monster. Questions would be raised about who the father was, and a vicious smear campaign against the ambitious Boleyn girl would sink her for good. Within three years of marriage, Henry allowed the execution of the woman he had referred to as his *'lovely wife'* just weeks before

Westminster Abbey, London

TUDOR TRAVEL

Let's imagine you've built a time machine. What would it be like to be on this route in 1535? You'll need to get about, and be able to hunt. Let's have a look at what's involved.

Road conditions

On your progress, you're travelling in your cosy metal chariot on smooth tarmacked roads. What would it have been like if you were travelling in the royal retinue in Tudor times?

The term *'road'* was coined a little later than the time of Henry's royal progress. It was in the Elizabethan era when it first appeared in print in the 1560s. Previously, terms like *'highway,' 'path,' 'lane,' 'street,'* and *'way,'* were more commonly used. Whatever you call them, these are among the oldest parts of the man-made landscape in the land.

Many of the Tudor routes you travel on date back to the time of the Romans. Even in a city where houses are constantly being built and rebuilt, the twists and turns of ancient paths linger like ghosts. Similarly, transportation along these roads remains constant.

On market day, you'll see hundreds of people approaching, driving cattle, sheep, or geese, with others leading carts loaded with sacks and crates. Some people will be walking with baskets on their arms or heads, holding them in place with a cushioning wreath of hay. Men carry large loads on their backs or lead slow packhorses burdened with panniers. In a way, it seems like modern life... until you hear the rumble of wheels behind you, the crack of the whip, and the speeding coachman's bellow for you to shift out of the way.

Unlike modern drivers, only the very rich could afford to buy or travel by stagecoach. A coach was an elaborate construction that would have cost several hundred pounds in the Middle Ages. In Henry's time, people started to think that simply having four wheels was enough. They could do away with carved, gilded woodwork and embroidered silk hangings.

In Elizabeth's time, a new coach in 1573 cost £34 14s. If you fancied painting a decal of your coat of arms on the side, that would be an extra 2s 6d. A second-hand vehicle could cost just a quarter of the new price. Before you get too excited about investing in a cheapo-coach, bear in mind you'll need a team of four or six horses to pull it. The price for feeding them can be a bit eye-watering, especially if you plan to stay in town. If you're travelling with servants, you will find the cost of feeding your steeds exceeds the costs of feeding your staff.

If you are male and bump into a Tudor man along the way, he may engage in a bit of banter, but he will think of you as *'effeminate'* for not riding on horseback. A workaround to this is to let the ladies of your household travel in a coach. You can ride alongside on your horse being the *'hero'*. Be aware that if your female loved ones are not visiting friends and family across the country, they will be off to the local Royal Exchange shopping centre in your coach, spending more of your money.

Coaches with four wheels are available for hire in London for 16s per day. Remember to budget for the driver's salary as well as horse feed. Keep in mind that if you stop at an inn and your driver learns that the road ahead

23

is extremely muddy, he may refuse to take your coach that way. On the rough roads, moving parts are easily damaged, and repairs are exorbitantly priced.

Do not lose your temper. The cart driver who refuses to attempt a tricky road is not being picky or pessimistic. Roads in Rome and medieval Europe were designed for light-footed pedestrians and animals rather than coaches with iron-tyred wheels that move more with as much haste and manoeuvrability as an oil tanker.

Another factor to consider is that most town roads are unpaved. Gravel is laid helpfully down at the worst-affected intersections to soak up the mud, but carts must otherwise pass through deep ruts of dried mud or try not to skid on soft wet soil. On *'paved'* Roman roads, stones near the surface are more likely to be a hazard than a help to a coachman. Landowners and tenants of land bordering highways are supposed to maintain the ditches that drain the roads, but this does not always happen. Things are left to slide into oblivion.

Literally, in some cases. People have been known to slip over into a ditch running alongside and drown. Once the road starts to deteriorate, it will take a lot of money to put it right, money that often isn't there.

Although the urban roads are in a better state of repair, driving a coach or cart through town is just as dangerous. Many people are forced to stack firewood in the street, sometimes beneath their eaves which sometimes blocks the thoroughfare. Despite many communities having bylaws prohibiting it, it remains a problem. On the streets, you'll see crates, tree branches and trunks, broken waggons in need of repair, split lumber, barrels, and troughs. As the cities' roads get clogged up with carriages, the locals complain about congestion and request limits to the number and type of vehicles permitted in the town centre. As well as congestion, there is the constant worry a cartman will fall asleep at the reins and run over pedestrians. Many men offering a *'taxi*

Example of a narrow medieval street in York

service' complain their livelihoods are being eroded as more people drive themselves rather than hire a professional coach or waterman.

The road itself is sometimes the victim of deliberate vandalism. For example, many urban folks dig in the streets for sand or clay to daub on their wattle structures, causing large potholes.

Carpenters' sawpits, which can be more than six feet deep, are no less dangerous. Be aware of the ones dug directly alongside the road to ease the offloading of hefty trunks close to where they will be cut into more manageable pieces.

There are fines for people who dig wells in or near roads, especially because citizens have a habit of falling into them and drowning.

Surveyors visit the parish and look for trouble spots in need of maintenance. Wealthy local parishioners are requested to supply labour and resources at set times, else face a fine for failing to contribute to the upkeep of the thoroughfares. Unfortunately, quite a few well-to-do folk send men and carts for a few days then pay the fines for the rest of the time, which slows the improvements.

The fundamental flaw in the Tudor road strategy is that those who are supposed to do all the work do not benefit significantly from it. Most labourers travel on foot or by horseback, and they have little need or desire to build roads for opulent coach passengers—hoity-toity wealthy women or *'effeminate'* men—or royal messengers. Most country dwellers simply walk around the quagmires in the winter and step over the hardened ruts in the summer. They can live with these impediments.

It will be economically impossible to maintain roadways adequately until the burden is imposed on the road user, which will take another century after Henry's death to implement.

Navigating

Tudor paper maps are far too large and expensive to transport. Furthermore, while they give you a good bird's eye view of the route, these maps are insufficiently detailed to guide you on the ground. More practical information in the form of printed tables shows the distances between towns and the directions you must follow to get there. Most of these tables are laid out in a circular pattern, with London at the centre and all other cities and towns radiating out in a series of concentric circles. The distance from the previous town is indicated in brackets. Other atlases, such as La Guide des Chemins d'Angleterre, are printed in French for the benefit of visitors from other countries. (Depending on how your French lessons went in school, this may or may not be useful.)

Of course, asking a kind stranger for directions is another option. Bear in mind, though, you may feel more anxious after asking. This is an example of a typical conversation.

> *Traveller: I'm hoping you can point me in the right direction to get to Reading.*
>
> *Ploughman: Continue straight past Windsor Castle until you reach a wooded corner, then turn left.*
>
> *Traveller: Are there robbers on the route?*
>
> *Ploughman: No, sir, because the provost-marshal just hanged a half-dozen thieves at the gibbet, which you can see at the top of that hill.*

With that information, you can only hope that those six were the most violent ringleaders. The number of desperate amateur vagabonds hiding behind trees and bushes to catch unsuspecting travellers off guard greatly increased due to vagrancy. Travellers note that thieves congregate on Gad's Hill near Rochester, Shooter's Hill near Blackheath, Newmarket Heath, which are not on your progress route—er, however, Salisbury Plain is.

These are just a few of the most well-known examples. On many Tudor highways, danger can lurk. Robberies often follow a pattern, which you will be well advised to learn.

You retire to bed after a night of ale-quaffing with your fellow travellers in a friendly inn. The inn's servants will note the visitors who have cash on the hip and eavesdrop on their intended direction of travel. When you leave the inn in the morning, they look to see how many people are in the party, and a messenger will go out ahead of you.

Your party will be crawling its way along an obstacle-laden path, navigating beneath overhanging trees and around muddy pot-holed stretches of road and the like when you will suddenly be confronted by men wielding swords, cudgels, possibly even basic long-barrelled guns. If you attempt to turn around, you will find that the path back to safety has also been blocked by their cohorts.

Now you realise you have two choices: live without your cash and valuables or fight to keep them. To time-travel forward to the Clint Eastwood era, *'Are you feeling lucky, punk?'*

Next, these highwaymen will take all your money and jewels, as well as any expensive clothing and horses. If you comply, they will tie you up away from the highway, but in such a way that you will be able to work yourself free after an hour or so of fierce struggle. If the worst should happen, take solace in the fact that you are not the first or last person to suffer this humiliation as you begin to walk to the next inn or town in nothing but your underwear—just as the rain starts.

Map from the 1570s

HUNTING WITH HAWKS

An ancient sport, hunting is a favourite pastime of the Tudors, dubbed *'the sport of royalty'* because the lower classes could not afford to participate. Falconry gives kings and lords the opportunity to host other nobles for grand hutting parties. Hawks are the most popular choice for bird hunting, whose prey were small wild game or birds. However, other birds are used, even eagles, on rare occasions.

Getting started

Before you take up the sport, go into it with your eyes open. It is not pocket-friendly. As well as cages, food, training, and a falconer to look after your feathered friends, there was an expensive list of accessories required to tame and hunt with a bird. You'll only want the finest leather hoods, gloves, leg jesses, bells, and lures for your pampered pets.

Your falconer, like his father before him, will put your bird through a rigorous training regimen, taking fledglings from their nests, after which their instruction begins. He will be responsible for capturing, training, and caring for it. Resist the temptation to be a cheapskate and *'pick your own'*. The nest sites are heavily guarded, and if you're caught, one of the punishments is blinding.

When it comes to selecting your falconer, during the interview process, to establish competency, ask what he will be teaching. He should respond *'how to return to captivity'*, rather than *'how to kill.'* Look for an early riser with good hearing, good eyesight, an even-temper, a loud calling voice. The ability to swim is a plus, and unlike others in the hunting fraternity, so is sobriety. Don't be tempted to cut corners. Employing the services of a falconer is crucial. If a hunting bird is to be reliable, it needs a lot of daily human contact and attention. The skill of the falconer is to train the hawk to hunt in partnership with its master-- you. You can't be a mover and shaker at court if you are seen in a field shouting: *'Right, that's it. I've told you time and time again!'* at a disobedient hawk. Equally, tramping the fields for hours to find your precious bird if it absconds impresses no one.

Falcon eating from a glove

Choosing your bird

Before you head to Birds-r-Us, there are lots of rules to choosing your bird depending on the sort of hunting you want to do and where you fit in the, er, social *'pecking'* order. To make the right choice, refer to the 1486 *'Boke of St Albans'*. It explains everything you need to know about selecting your bird. Available in full colour, it's one of the first examples of a printed colour book in England. It discusses hawking, hunting, heraldry.

As monarchs, both Henry and Anne hunt with falcons. You won't. Skim this list and see what you can bring.

King: Gyrfalcon
Largest, strongest, and noblest of the falcons. Achieves greater heights with less effort. Native to Greenland, Iceland, or Scandinavia.

Prince: Peregrine falcon
Favourite of falconers. Circles high overhead waiting for the quarry to be flushed, then dives at 200 mph.

Duke: Rock falcon
A subspecies of the peregrine. Brown, medium-sized, slender bird weighing about 300g.

Earl: Tiercel peregrine falcon
Smaller male bird, about a third of the size of a female.

Baron: Common buzzard
They don't manoeuvre well in the air. Can be forced to the ground and killed by groups of jackdaws, crows, and ravens. Urgh.

Knight: Saker
The Arab falconer's choice. Hardier than peregrines, but not useful for river quarry.

Squire: Lanner
Popular in France and Spain. Pros: good for partridges, herons, hares. Cons: need to be flown in pairs.

Lady: Female merlin
Like miniature peregrines. Feisty. Capable of taking down quarry as large as themselves.

Yeoman: Goshawk or hobby
Go for a Goshawk. Grouchy but good food producers: partridges, pheasants, hares. Hawks of the fist. Can get by without hooding. Hobbies tend to eat insects rather than hunt birds in the air. Handy first bird for your lad.

Priest/Holy water clerks: Sparrowhawk
Unpredictable. Known to keel over and die for no apparent reason. Avoid.

Knaves, servants, kids: Kestrel
Looks impressive. Hovers over prey by fanning wings before striking on the ground, never in the air.

If you can't see where you fit into these groups, to avoid making a social faux-pas and make a profit on your trip, look for trained birds that have flown off. If you can capture one, you can sell it on the second-hand market for a good price.

Understanding your bird

Lithe, longer-winged birds catch prey in the air, such as other birds. They are well suited to open moorland where the engagement is easy to observe. The shorter and broader winged varieties are good for the ground game, such as rabbits or pheasants. These birds are more used to forests and hunting from trees. Naturally suited to perching, they are comfortable on a gloved fist.

You'll find different birds also have different temperaments, which influence their suitability for training. For example, some birds will welcome a hood. It keeps them relaxed in an environment where they might otherwise be nervous. Some birds are well suited to a novice handler. Others can only be controlled by an expert hunter.

Training, diet, and exercise

Your falconer trains the hawk to perch on his fist by feeding morsels of meat from his gloved hand. This is called *'manning'*. It literally means getting used to human handling. The next step is encouraging the bird to fly to the fist to earn a reward.

Like hiring a personal trainer at the gym, the level of activity and the amount of edible rewards given needed careful management to make sure your bird doesn't put on too much weight. Body composition and nutrition is carefully monitored to optimise your bird's hunting potential.

The aim is to match their *'wild weight'* as much as possible to their weight in captivity. Like an athlete, your bird will be kept fighting fit by increasing the time it spends flying and the distances covered before it is called back. If your bird doesn't have an appetite, it is less likely to follow its orders. The hungrier a bird becomes, the greater the distance it will cover for the reward.

Prey in flight is simulated by tying a pair of bird's wings to a long lure and swinging them through the air. Ask to see your bird's detailed training records. These will show if the training is effective. Until the bird is obedient, it will be tethered as it flies. During the training, you might see your falconer sewing your bird's eyes closed to help it do as it's told. Don't panic. The lids will open and close again when the thread is adjusted as needed.

Once the initial training is second nature, the falconer will dispense with the tether, and your bird will be introduced to wild game. He'll check that when released, instinctively, your bird will seek out its quarry. It should sink its talons into the flesh and bring it back to the falconer.

If your bird tends to be a little too *'lively'*, your falconer will add jesses, leather straps to the legs. It makes retaining your trainee feathered friend on the glove much easier. It also means they can be released when specific game is sighted.

When your bird returns, it'll be distracted with food on the glove. It forgets about the quarry, giving your falconer time to snaffle it into the game bag. This also stops your bird gorging on the meat, so it'll retain its sleek figure. Plus, since it'll still feel, er, peckish, it will be chipper about being sent off again for another kill.

Should the bird abscond, the bells attached give you some hope it will be found. As a modern falconer, you might want to tag yours with an electronic transmitter.

Organising the hunt

Hooded birds are released when the quarry was spotted by the hunter, i.e., you. This is called *'out of the hood.'*

Much like shooting fish in a barrel, men with sticks and highly trained hounds can flush out the prey from their hiding places. This is called *'waiting on'*. Hover your bird above the area, then watch it dive down into the prepared area below. If you need to reposition your bird, you or your falconer walk in a direction and the bird should follow. This can be backed up with audible instructions to change course. Resist the temptations to swear at your bird. Rather, give it the precise whistles it has been taught to recognise.

Tip: If you want some insider knowledge, Henry's hawking glove and one of the hoods are exhibited at Oxford's Ashmolean Museum.

PRIOR TO DEPARTURE
WINDSOR
JUL 1535

POSTCODE: SL4 1NJ (WINDSOR CASTLE)

Home to British royalty for centuries, rich in history and royal tradition, and home to the world's oldest and largest inhabited castle.

Henry VIII's gate at Windsor Castle, Berkshire

Windsor Castle

Windsor Castle was one of Henry's most important residences. The main entrance is the archway bearing his name, rebuilt around 1511 and is now the modern-day visitors' gateway into this magnificent building. The king visited Windsor regularly and enjoyed hunting in the surrounding forests. His first wife, Catherine of Aragon, was imprisoned in Windsor while her husband was negotiating the annulment of their marriage. Henry Fitzroy, Henry's illegitimate son, also lived here for a time.

Windsor is the home of the Order of the Garter, which is headquartered at St George's Chapel. The Most Noble Order of the Garter is a chivalric order. It was founded in 1348 by the English king, Edward III. It is the most senior order of knighthood in the British honours system, and in modern times outranked only the George and the Victoria Crosses in precedence.

Henry had been made a Knight of the Garter by his father around 1495, but as monarch, he became head of the order and appointed several of his courtiers as Knights of the Garter, including Henry Guildford and William Fitzwilliam, both of whom Holbein depicted proudly wearing their Garter collars. The Black Book of the Garter, a lavish register of the order, depicts Henry enthroned and surrounded by his knights.

During Henry's reign, St George's Chapel was completed, and he chose to be buried there with his favourite wife, his third, Jane Seymour. (He is rumoured to have met her for the first time, later on the progress at Wolf Hall, the vestiges of which you'll visit later). Although the magnificent tomb he envisioned was never completed, a ledger stone in the quire marks the location of his burial.

Henry departed for his tour from Windsor Castle, heading for Reading by the 9th of July, to be welcomed by Hugh Faringdon, abbot of the abbey. You might wish to stay in Windsor a little longer. There are some fabulous things to do here.

Visiting

There are plenty of central, long stay car parks in Windsor. If you prefer to travel in by train, there are direct trains from Slough to Windsor and Eton Central or South West London to Windsor and Eton Riverside.

Windsor attractions

Windsor Castle

Castle Hill, Windsor SL4 1PD
www.royalcollection.org.uk/visit/windsorcastle

No trip to Windsor would be complete without a visit to the magnificent Windsor Castle, which has served as the family home of British kings and queens for over 1,000 years. The size of the Castle (13 acres) is breathtaking; in fact, it is the world's largest and oldest occupied Castle, and it is where Queen Elizabeth enjoyed the majority of her private weekends.

Look at the flag flying from the Round Tower of the castle. If it's the Royal Standard, which is made up of (4

31

distinct panals with lions and a harp) the monarch will be there too.

Included in the ticket is a visit to St George's chapel where Henry was buried with third wife, Jane Seymour.

Photo: Michael Garlick

Dorney Court

Dorney Court Court Lane Windsor SL4 6QP
www.dorneycourt.co.uk

One of the finest Tudor manor houses in England. It was built around 1440 and has been inhabited by the same family since 1540. Excellent architecture, as well as a fine collection of portraits and furniture dating from the 16th to the 20th centuries. It is a rare surviving 'gentry' house that has remained remarkably unchanged. It's right next to the village church. With over 5,000 plants, the walled garden's cafe serves light lunches and cream teas.

Fudge Kitchen

20 Thames St, Windsor SL4 1PL
www.fudgekitchen.co.uk

A unique and unforgettable experience. Have some fun making fudge and getting your hands sticky, then sample a variety of flavours and take some fudge home. Prebook a time-slot and participate in a fudge-making demonstration with a confectionery expert who will explain how to make delicious fudge.

Eton College and Museums

Eton High St, Windsor SL4 6DW
collections.etoncollege.com

On Sunday afternoons, the collection museums are open. Start your visit at the Museum of Eton Life, where you can travel back in time and learn about life at the school since its inception in the 1400s. Then, cross School Yard to see the latest temporary exhibition in the Verey Gallery, which features objects and art from our collections as well as loans from other places. Then, walk a short distance to the Natural History Museum, where you can learn more about the natural world. Finish your visit with a visit to the Museum of Antiquities, where you can see objects from the ancient world and learn more about life in Ancient Egypt.

The Long Walk

The Long Walk, Windsor SL4 1BP
www.windsorgreatpark.co.uk

The Long Walk is arguably Windsor Great Park's most well-known image.

32

At the far end, it runs all the way to Windsor Castle. This tree-lined avenue leads down to the ancient fortress, demonstrating Windsor Great Park's royal heritage and grandeur.

Windsor Great Park

Rangers Gate, Windsor SL4 2LD
www.windsorgreatpark.co.uk

Windsor Great Park dates back to pre-Saxon times. It the 13th century the area was formerly defined. The 4,800 acres that have grown and been developed over time have created an incredible variety of landscapes. Wandering through the Great Park, you'll come across royal residences, formal gardens, and trees that have been standing for over 1,000 years. From William I's use of the landscape as a hunting ground a thousand years ago, to Charles II's original planting of the Long Walk, Queen Victoria entertaining on the shores of Virginia Water, to HRH the Duke of Edinburgh's stewardship as Ranger of the Great Park for nearly 70 years, the landscape's Rroyal connections have remained strong throughout the years.

The Long Walk, Windsor

STOP 1
READING
WED 9 JUL 1535

POSTCODE: RG1 3EH (FORBURY GARDENS)

Reading Abbey was founded by Henry I in 1121. Now a picturesque ruin, it was once one of the richest abbeys in medieval Britain

Lion at Forbury Gardens, the former site of Reading Abbey

Reading Abbey

The glittering train of the royal progress, probably a mile to a mile and a half long, left Windsor on its first leg of the tour, on its way to Reading Abbey, a longer journey of just under eighteen miles. If walked at a steady pace in good weather, the procession route could have been completed in about six hours. Allowing for stops, the journey would have taken between eight and nine hours. In July in England, daylight lasts well beyond nine o'clock in the evening, so it lends itself to a long, slow tempo.

The twelfth-century monastery was founded by William the Conqueror's youngest son, Henry I. During his travels, Henry frequented monastic houses because they were expected to provide hospitality. Feeding the hungry and sheltering the wayfarer were two of the seven '*Acts of Mercy*', fundamental Christian obligations (along with giving water to the thirsty, clothing the naked, visiting the sick, visiting prisoners, or ransomed captives and burying the dead.)

Reading Abbey was one of the six wealthiest monasteries in England during Henry's reign, and it was a favourite of the king's, appearing on his itinerary regularly. This was not Anne's first visit either; she had accompanied the king and court when they stayed on their way to Woodstock in July 1529 and Windsor in August 1532.

The abbot's house itself was used to house important guests. In Henry's time, the monastic 'inner sanctum' was not open to the public, unlike the open space within the abbey walls. At Reading, the abbot's former residence stood beside the inner gateway. In 1535, Anne would have been housed in one of the king and queen's sumptuous guest rooms. Unfortunately, the abbey would not be able to accommodate all the members of court. The remainder would have stayed in the town itself. The once-glorious abbey church, close to the size of the current St Paul's in London, is now in a ruin in Forbury Gardens, a distant echo of its former self. Unfortunately, the exact location of the abbot's house where Anne stayed is unknown. It survived the Dissolution only to be destroyed in 1642 during the English Civil War.

The public areas within the abbey held frequent markets, fairs, or religious celebrations where monks and townspeople could freely interact, and this space now forms the modern public park. The abbey gateway and the main building of the hospitium, a pilgrimage guest house, both survive, albeit in heavily restored condition.

The abbey ruins were stripped of their stone facing and thus lack any former decorative embellishments; however, several beautifully carved fragments are exhibited at Reading Museum and give a sense of the former richness of the buildings.

The Abbot, Hugh Faringdon, is an interesting character who came to a grisly end at the hands of Cromwell.

Born Hugh Cook, around 1500, he took the surname Faringdon (a local town near Reading) when he became a monk. Thought to have been educated within the abbey. Faringdon kept the abbey in good order. After his schooling, later, he worked in the abbey cellar, responsible for supplies and stores and before his election as abbot, in 1520, he was the abbey's sub-chamberlain, responsible for clothing and bedding. Supporting the abbey's grammar school was another of his interests. It had a good reputation and attracted professional staff and noble students. He was also trusted to serve in local government as a Justice of the Peace.

Despite his personal opposition to Protestant ideas, as evidenced by his refusal to allow anyone associated with these new opinions to be attached to the abbey, he consistently supported the government as a member of the House of Lords. He signed petitions to the pope to support Henry's divorce, even offering to scour the abbey's library books for more evidence. Hugh frequently entertained Henry at the abbey, who dubbed him *'his own abbot'* before appointing him as his Royal Chaplain in 1532. Also, that year, Henry gave the abbot twenty pounds, presented in a white leather purse. When the king was hunting in the area, Hugh would send him gifts of Kennet trout or hunting knives.

In 1536, Faringdon took the Royal Supremacy oath and agreed to the dissolution of the minor monasteries. He sang a requiem mass at Jane Seymour's funeral in 1537. In 1538 he was still appointed as a Justice of the Peace. Despite all this royal support, the abbot was deposed quickly in 1539, after Faringdon refused to comply with hints to dissolve Reading Abbey. When the commissioners arrived to take its surrender, they reported favourably on the abbot's willingness to conform, but the surrender of the abbey does not survive, and it is, therefore, unknown whether Faringdon signed it.

Faringdon was charged with high treason in 1539, accused of providing financial assistance to the Northern rebels and taken to the Tower, where he was imprisoned for two months. As a mitred abbot, he was entitled to a trial by Parliament, but Chancellor Cromwell chose not to wait for that. Faringdon's death sentence was passed before his trial even began. Found guilty, he was hanged, drawn, and quartered before the inner abbey gatehouse on 14 November 1539.

After a morning departure, the royal train wended its way to the next stop, Ewelme Palace, a 15-mile journey.

Visiting

The ruins of the former abbey are at Forbury Gardens. Reading station is a good place to park as it's well sign-posted and close to the gardens.

Reading attractions

Reading Museum

Blagrave St, Reading RG1 1QH
www.readingmuseum.org.uk

Housed in the Victorian town hall, the museum is in the heart of the city. Discover our Huntley & Palmers biscuit tin collection, Roman Silchester and Reading Abbey archaeology, the famous Victorian copy of the Bayeux Tapestry, Reading's natural history, modern art and sculpture, and much more.

Photo: Chris Wood

The Oracle Shopping Centre

The Oracle Centre, Reading RG1 2AG
www.theoracle.com

Step back into modern times and enjoy the shopping at the Oracle close to Reading's retail heart. Stop for food and drinks at the wide selection of waterside bars and eateries.

Photo: Museum of English Rural Life

Museum of English Rural Life

6 Redlands Rd, Reading Univ, Reading RG1 5EX
merl.reading.ac.uk

Explore the immersive galleries, relax in the garden, and grab a bite to eat at the café. This museum houses the most comprehensive national collection of objects, books, and archives relating to the history of food, farming, and the countryside.

Silchester Roman City Walls and Amphitheatre

Wall Lane, Reading RG7 2HP
www.english-heritage.org.uk

From the late 1st century BC, Silchester was the capital of the Atrebates tribe's Iron Age kingdom. Following the Roman conquest, it grew into the town of Calleva Atrebatum. The town thrived until the early Anglo-Saxon period. Silchester, was extensively excavated and is one of the best preserved Roman towns in Britain.

TimeTrap Escape Rooms

11 Friar St, Reading RG1 1DB
www.timetrapescaperooms.com

Immersive escape room adventures in the heart of Reading. Be transported back in time to rewrite history at the Great Fire of London, WWII's Bletchley Park, and more.

Market Square, Reading, Berkshire

STOP 2
EWELME PALACE
SUN 12 JUL 1535

POSTCODE: OX10 6HP (ST MARY'S CHURCH)

The palace has long gone, but St Mary's is connected with Geoffrey Chaucer, whose son, Thomas and his wife Matilda are buried there.

Ewelme, Oxfordshire

Ewelme Palace

The property, a royal retreat at the time, was seized by Henry's father following the downfall of the previous owner, Richard III's nephew, Edmund de la Pole. He was next-in-line to the throne via the Plantagenet line. Initially imprisoned for his Yorkist sympathies by Henry VII, Henry VIII had him beheaded on 30 April 1513 after seven years in the Tower of London. Within 12 months, the earl's confiscated estates and titles were given to Charles Brandon, newly created Duke of Suffolk and one of the king's favourite companions.

Twelve years later, in 1525, Ewelme was granted to Henry's sister Mary, now Brandon's wife. After Mary died in 1533, Suffolk remarried. However, by 1535, Charles's lack of enthusiasm for Henry's marriage to Anne was repaid with his temporary fall from favour, and the king asked for the property back in exchange for lands elsewhere.

Henry and Anne inspected the manor on July 12 and 13, 1535. The duke claimed to have spent £1,000 on Ewelme, but the royal couple were unimpressed. When the King himself viewed Ewelme when recently there, '*he found the manor in great decay*' and in need of large sums of money to repair it.

Nonetheless, Ewelme became a royal residence once more, and the king used it as a lesser house, a place where he could retreat for greater privacy with a select group of friends while on hunting trips.

By the reign of James I, the '*capital mansion*' had decayed completely.

Around the time the king reached Ewelme, the king's commissioners also set out for the West Country, led by Richard Layton, Thomas Leigh, John Prise, and John London. Their mission, known as the '*Valor Ecclesiasticus*', was to visit and appraise church property. This work would ultimately result in destroying the monastic buildings that Anne Boleyn desperately wanted to save.

A friendlier face for Anne than Cromwell and his cohorts was Sir Henry Norris, the bailiff at Ewelme. Henry became one of Anne Boleyn's closest allies and the faction leader who supported her proud ambition while gaining her position at court.

During his youth, Norris became a close friend of Henry, who appointed him a Gentleman of the Bedchamber and granted him many offices thereafter. In 1520, he attended the Field of the Cloth of Gold meeting between Henry and King Francis I of France. In 1526, Norris took over as Groom of the Stool, responsible for the king's personal hygiene, an intimate and trusted role. In 1535, he received a few manors previously held by the recently executed Sir Thomas More.

Although Norris's initial support of Wolsey around the time of his fall had angered the Boleyn clique, his assistance of Anne as she established her position at court meant he had become one of her close friends as well as the leader of the faction that supported her attempts to wield political power. This support put him at odds with Cromwell, who was becoming increasingly irritated with Anne's opinions on the Dissolution. Within months of the visit to the tranquil hamlet of Ewelme, both Norris and Anne would be dead.

Visiting

Ewelme is yet another picturesque rural setting on the tour. The manor house hasn't survived. However, other interesting structures have.

Over twenty years, William and Alice de la Pole rebuilt the church, established the almshouse, and created the school, which still stand as a testament to the splendour of the de la Poles' former estate.

The current Parish church, St Mary's (OX10 6HP), is about a half-mile uphill from the original manor house. The house where Henry and Anne stayed had its own private chapel. This makes it tricky to establish if the royal couple visited in person but undoubtedly saw it as they embarked on their frequent hunting trips.

You can also see Ewelme School (OX10 6HU) from the road.

Close stool from Hampton Court c.1650

Watercress farm at Ewelme

STOP 3
ABINGDON
TUE 14 JUL 1535

POSTCODE: OX14 3HZ (THAMES STREET)

Abingdon-on-Thames, a quaint, bustling market town nestled on the river just waiting to be explored, six miles south of Oxford.

St Mary's Church, Abingdon. Oxfordshire

Abingdon Abbey

Henry and Anne made the 10-mile journey from Ewelme to Abingdon, a convenient stopping point with a river crossing en route to Langley. It wasn't their first visit. The couple also enjoyed the hospitality of this great monastic house eleven months earlier. The approach into town across Abingdon Bridge must have offered them a good view of the spire of the nearby, late medieval St Helen's church that still dominates the town's skyline. Back then, the towers of the abbey would have been visible too.

The abbot of the time, Thomas Rowland, would have welcomed his royal guests with great pageantry and housed them in the abbot's home, a large mansion with sumptuous guest rooms, spacious halls, offices, and its own kitchen.

Although nothing of this former residence remains today, a few buildings that Anne would have seen at the time of her visit still do.

The main abbey gateway was rebuilt around 1450 and is still standing. St Nicholas' church was built in 1184 for the abbey's servants and lay tenants. The former St John's hospital, founded as a lay infirmary, The latter was constructed around 1130 and is one of Abingdon's oldest structures.

The old hospital ward, used as the magistrate's court today, first became a courtroom after the Dissolution.

A second group of buildings, the bakehouse, the Checker Hall, and the long gallery, still standing in Henry's day, are on Thames Street.

What was once a part of the monastic bakehouse is now the office of the Friends of Abingdon, the group in charge of rescuing, restoring, and maintaining these historic structures.

The Checker Hall now houses an Elizabethan-style stage and the Unicorn Theatre.

After Sir Richard Rich surveyed the vast complex of buildings, courtyards, and gardens, he wrote to Cromwell saying that he wished him to *'signify to the king's majesty that many of the houses of office thereof be much in ruin and decay except the church... and as concerning the abbot's lodgings, I think it is not like a royal house'*.

In February 1538, the abbey was the first of the larger monasteries to be dissolved. Within weeks, a team of thirty-two men arrived to remove the lead and stone from the abbey church. Many of the buildings were demolished.

During Lent 1535, Cromwell wrote to Abbot Thomas requesting that the auditors examine the accounts. There had been a long-running argument between the abbot and the abbey steward, John Audelette.

The abbot wrote asking that it be postponed until the commissioners were to sit between him and Audelett in June, hoping that the matter would be settled before the king and Cromwell left Abingdon. It wasn't. The dispute dragged on for a long time, with the steward putting up every obstacle. Only Audelett's death in November 1536 ended it.

Meanwhile, Dr Leyton, Cromwell's commissary for the *'Valor Ecclesiastica'*, visited Abingdon and issued the familiar injunction confining the monks to their precincts all year round.

The long-running lawsuit with their steward and Cromwell's increasing demands had embarrassed the abbot and convent. They had finally *'surrendered'*.

Despite Leigh and Layton accusing the abbot of numerous sinful transgressions, including fathering children incestuously, the abbot was granted a large pension and was allowed to live in the Cumnor manor house for the rest of his life.

Principal agents of Henry and Cromwell, John Tregonwell and Sir William Petre, received a large sum of money on 7 February 1538 to manage the dissolution. Within weeks, a team of thirty-two men arrived to remove the valuable lead and stone from the abbey church, and most of the buildings were demolished from there.

Visiting

Although not much of Abingdon Abbey remains today, the surviving buildings and ancient grounds are a reminder of happier times, when Abingdon was one of the greatest monasteries in England, and Anne Boleyn was still the king's *'most beloved wife'*.

Thames Street and the abbey gardens are open to the public at all reasonable times, but the abbey buildings have set opening times and may be closed for private functions, so it's best to check the Friends of Abingdon abbey website before visiting.

Website:

- abingdonabbeybuildings.co.uk

Fifteenth-century Abbey Gateway, Abingdon, Oxfordshire

STOP 4

KING JOHN'S PALACE LANGLEY

THU 16 JULY 1535

POSTCODE: OX29 9QD (W3W:///DEFINITE.CURLY.INSERT)

Now gone, Henry loved this palace and was a frequent visitor, revelling in the privacy it offered just as much as the hunting.

King John (1166 – 1216)

Langley, Oxfordshire

The court had travelled 12 miles from Abingdon Abbey to the small hamlet of Langley, on the high ground to the south of Shipton-under-Wychwood. They stayed for five days. The manor's location was rumoured to be the site of a palace of King John.

The Neville family owned the Langley manor in the 1400s. In 1478, Isabelle Neville, the elder daughter of Richard Neville, 16th Earl of Warwick and the legendary 'Kingmaker' of the Wars of the Roses, died.

The manor passed to her husband, George Plantagenet, Duke of Clarence, who died the same year. It then reverted to crown property. Henry VII was a frequent visitor and, beginning in 1496, oversaw much of the construction work. He loved the hunting grounds around Wychwood Forest and its close proximity to his impressive palace at Woodstock, Oxfordshire.

Henry loved the place and was a frequent visitor, revelling in its privacy as much as the hunting.

Meeting Sir Francis Weston

On a visit three years earlier, Henry was given 100 crowns to play dice, which he lost to Sir Francis Weston. Francis was the son of Sir Richard Weston, a prominent courtier and diplomat for Henry. Young 15-year-old Francis became a court page in 1526.

Despite being twenty years younger than the king, he quickly became a minor member of Henry's circle. Athletic, delighting in playing bowls and tennis with the king and playing the lute and gambling, he was a member of the rising Boleyn faction and a popular man of the king's court.

In 1532, a promotion to Gentleman of the Privy Chamber gave him close access to Henry. Weston was often chosen to sleep in the King's bedchamber and attend to the king's every whim. Anne and George Boleyn also thought of him as a favourite.

Sir Francis Weston (likely portrait)

Other honours followed for Francis, including becoming a Knight of the Bath at Anne's coronation in 1533. A fascinating investiture process, it began the night before the actual knighting ceremony.

The men were to first take a bath to cleanse their bodies of any impurities. This washing was inspired by the idea of baptism, which washed away the sins of the soul. After bathing, they were carefully dried and dressed in a robe. They would then proceed to the chapel to keep vigil for the night. When dawn arrived, the future knight would attend mass and make his confessions. He would then be presented to the sovereign, and whilst kneeling, would be given his ceremonial spurs and a belt.

The king would then tap him on the head with his hand or a sword, making him a Knight of the Bath.

Visiting

The building has changed significantly since it entered private ownership. It is not open to the public. Known as Langley Farm and extensively remodelled in 1858, it retains some of its fifteenth-, sixteenth-, and eighteenth-century architecture, including Tudor walls.

The initials H E, for Henry VII and Elizabeth of York, can still be seen on a stone panel at the front of the farmhouse.

Although the stunning formal gardens have been replaced with pasture, pockets of Wychwood Forest can be found around the nearby town of Charlbury. (Postcode: OX7 3PW)

Arable land around Charlbury and Wychwood Forest

STOP 5
SUDELEY CASTLE
TUE 21 JUL 1535

POSTCODE: GL54 5JD (CASTLE)

With royal connections spanning a millennium, Sudeley Castle has played a key role in the turbulent times of England's past.

Sudeley Castle, Gloucestershire

Sudeley and Winchcombe

The journey from Langley to Winchcombe was around 15 miles for the winding royal train. The immediate retinue stayed at Sudeley Castle a further five miles away, while the rest of the court stayed at nearby Winchcombe and its abbey. The procession trundled through the Cotswolds' rolling hills where the wool merchants' wealth was concentrated but by then a declining industry. The court was always near a 'wool church', a house of God built with money from wool merchants and farmers' profits over the preceding centuries.

They crossed the Roman Fosse Way at some point on this stretch, most likely at Stow-on-the-Wold. From there, they would travel through villages made of picturesque, buttery Cotswold stone, many of which have remained largely unchanged to this day.

The royal train edged its way down the steep hill into Winchcombe with an hour of daylight remaining. As it appears today, Sudeley Castle is mostly Elizabethan, built in the late sixteenth century and partially restored in the mid-nineteenth. The castle Henry visited dated from the 1400s with work continuing into the 1470s, undertaken by Richard, Duke of Gloucester. The more opulent apartments, where Anne almost certainly stayed, appear to have been in the now-ruined east range of the inner court, probably constructed by Richard. Like many royal residences, it is steeped in history, intrigue, deceit, and betrayal.

Besides Anne, several other royals are associated with Sudeley. Lady Jane Grey, queen for nine days, lived at the castle, as did Thomas Seymour, Queen Jane's brother. Henry's sixth and last wife, Katherine Parr, who outlived the king, took Thomas Seymour to be her fourth husband. She is buried in Sudeley's chapel after dying in childbirth in 1549.

Katherine's tomb.

In the fight with his brother Edward and the regency council over the control of nine-year-old King Edward VI, Thomas Seymour was executed the same year for treason. His crime, along with several rumours of impropriety with his step-daughter Elizabeth, was found outside the young king's bedchamber at Hampton Court Palace armed with a gun. Whether he planned to kill him or abscond with the lad was hotly debated.

King Edward VI

48

On or around 23 July, Thomas Cromwell joined the court, lodging at Winchcombe. While under the abbey's roof, as well as dealing with the day-to-day business of government, Thomas met with his agents and briefed them on more injunctions—created in consultation with the king—that would be issued to the monks following an abbey's inspection.

Cromwell's henchmen fanned out from Winchcombe and *'visited'* several monastic houses, while Anne's disapproving gaze fell on a nearby religious house called Hailes Abbey, irritated by the large amount of reliquary stored there. Clauses in the injunctions prohibited the *'display of relics or feigned miracles.'*

While she was staying at Sudeley, Anne dispatched her chaplain, William Latymer and possibly John Hilsey, to the nearby abbey, two miles northeast of Winchcombe. Their mission was to investigate an infamous relic of the holy blood of Christ, which had transformed the abbey into one of the most popular pilgrimage sites in late medieval England since a crucifixion relic proved to be quite a draw.

Through the resulting pilgrim proceeds, the monks of Hailes were able to rebuild the abbey on a magnificent scale. Henry's commissioners declared the famous relic to be *'nothing but the blood of a duck'* that was regularly renewed. Abbot Stephen Sagar admitted it was a hoax in the hope of saving the abbey. His strategy failed. Putting an end to the *'abuse'* of the relic was a perfect opportunity for Henry to demonstrate his reforming zeal.

Although Hailes was one of the last religious abbeys to acquiesce, the abbot and his monks finally surrendered on Christmas Eve 1539. The abbey was gradually demolished over the years, leaving only an outline today, a shadowy reminder of where many pilgrims' feet had sought an encounter with the divine. Hailes Abbey represents the end of popular medieval devotion and the beginnings of an age in which people were less willing to accept the clergy's pronouncements on trust alone.

Aside from sending representatives to Hailes, Henry and Anne planned to visit the abbey, though it is unclear whether they did.

Neighbouring Winchcombe Abbey would suffer a similar fate. Despite its power and elegance, Cromwell's grip was tightening around it too. Rules were soon imposed. Abbot Mounslow, like Abbot Roland in Abingdon, did not like them. He and the convent also petitioned Cromwell to change some of the more draconian ones, banning the community from leaving the buildings, accepting visitors, or helping people in need.

Visiting

For up to date information, visit the website. Sudeley is not open all year round, so check before visiting.

Website:

- www.sudeleycastle.co.uk

Winchcombe attractions

Winchcombe

High Street, Winchcombe, Cheltenham, GL54 5LJ
www.winchcombe.co.uk

A pretty little village, the history of Winchcombe is a long one, beginning in the Neolithic period, when people settled in the hills and left a stone-lined burial chamber – the Belas Knap long barrow. It was a royal centre favoured by Mercian kings in Saxon times, and in the Middle Ages it became a pilgrimage site and thriving wool town. During the Victorian era, it expanded with a town hall,

Hailes Abbey

Cotswold Way, Hailes, Cheltenham GL54 5PB
www.english-heritage.org.uk

Hailes Abbey, founded in 1246 by the Earl of Cornwall, is now the tranquil ruins of the former entre of monastic life. An ideal place to relax and enjoy a picnic in a unique historic setting. Discover the treasures of Hailes at the museum, which tells the stories of the monks who lived and worshipped at the abbey for nearly three centuries.

Winchombe village, Gloucestershire

STOP 6
TEWKESBURY
SUN 26 JUL 1535

POSTCODE: GL20 5RZ (TEWKESBURY ABBEY)

A rich heritage spanning more than 1,000 years with half-timbered medieval houses, an abbey and Tudor buildings.

Tewkesbury Abbey, Gloucestershire

Tewkesbury Abbey

On Monday, the royal party left Sudeley Castle and travelled 7 miles northwest towards Tewkesbury, listed as the most northerly point on the route. There is no record of where the royal party stayed in Tewkesbury, despite staying for several days. They were three days behind schedule but weren't in any hurry to make up the time. None of the stops was omitted thus far. Staying roughly for the time specified in the original geists meant four days in Tewkesbury.

According to a letter from Cromwell on 29 July and signed from *'The Monastery of Tewkesbury,'* Henry and Anne would have been escorted to their lodgings. After making an offering at the church, this was most likely within the most distinguished accommodation within the abbey precincts. On their arrival, the mayor and other local dignitaries would have greeted the king, queen, and their entourage just outside town, with the two parties merging to travel in procession to the cathedral or abbey church.

Although work on the abbey started at the time of the Norman invasion, Tewkesbury had been rebuilt in the early sixteenth century and was thus relatively new when the royal party visited. Although some of the abbey buildings were destroyed after the Dissolution, the abbot's lodgings were preserved and are now part of Abbey House. (These days, the house is the home of the current Vicar of Tewkesbury.) So close to the abbey's main entrance, it allowed the Abbot, John Wiche, to greet all his guests, including Anne, when she arrived.

Tewkesbury's bridge over the River Avon still bears King John's name, and his body is buried a few miles away in Worcester Cathedral. Although he died in Newark-on-Trent, Nottinghamshire, he chose to be buried near the shrine of his patron saint, Wulfstan. Prince Arthur, Henry's older brother, was also buried in the cathedral in 1502.

In 1471, during the Wars of the Roses, Henry Tudor fled to Brittany from there. Later, in 1485, he returned through Wales and the west of England, gathering support to defeat Richard III at Bosworth, Leicestershire and finally proclaimed the kingdom for himself.

Visiting

The abbey is open all year round and has a dedicated website with more details. Entry is free, but it is suggested visitors leave a donation.

Website:

- www.tewkesburyabbey.org.uk

STOP 7
GLOUCESTER
FRI 31 JUL 1535

> **POSTCODE: GL1 2LX (GLOUCESTER CATHEDRAL)**

Nestled between the Cotswolds and the Forest of Dean, Britain's most inland port is rich with history dating back to Roman times.

Gloucester docks and the cathedral, Gloucestershire

Gloucester Abbey

Gloucester is around ten miles south of Tewkesbury, and the road runs parallel to the River Severn, allowing for downriver boat travel. Henry's court spent almost the entire month of August in Gloucestershire. Unlike other stops on the progress, this was Henry's first visit to the city since his coronation. A detailed account of their arrival survived.

The royal couple were greeted by the mayor John Falconer as well as '*aldermen, sheriffs, and about* 100 *or so burgesses of the town of Gloucester.*' The party rode out wearing their finest clothes. They met the king and queen close to the modern site of Down Hatherley village, where they bowed on horseback, offering the king their right hands in turn. The mayor then kissed the town mace and delivered a long speech which began:

'*God bless your Grace's health and prosperity, which may he keep for a long time!*'

The royal entourage then passed by Whitefriars (the remains of which were recently discovered when a multi-storey car park was redeveloped), just outside the city walls before arriving at the medieval Northgate, at the northern end of the current Lower North Gate Street.

Here, they were greeted by clergymen dressed in their copes and carrying crosses, carpets, and cushions. The royal couple stopped to kiss a cross, then made their way along College Street, known then as St Edwardes Lane.

When Henry and Anne dismounted, they entered the abbey precinct and were greeted in the porch by Abbot Parker and his brethren, all wearing their rich ceremonial garb.

Anne and Henry dismounted, and both kneeled and kissed the cross once more with great reverence, then went up to the high altar. From there, they retired to their accommodation, probably the abbot's lodgings, close to the cathedral and on its northern side, facing modern-day Pitt Street. They were often seen in the abbey's yard before preparing to leave for a day's hunting prior to their departure on 7 August.

Visiting

Gloucester city centre is compact and easy to walk around. Waterwells Park and Ride, Telford Way, Quedgeley, GL2 2AB, and lots of car parks make visiting easy.

Gloucester attractions

International Centre for Birds of Prey

Boulsdon House, Newent GL18 1JJ
www.icbp.org

Home to over 200 birds of prey. Daily, for over 50 years the centre has given three flying. Explore the gardens and woodland, eat at the cafe, and see everything from pygmy falcons to Steller's sea eagles! Get a good idea of the birds Henry and Anne would be familiar with.

Briery Hill Llamas

Briery Hill Lane Kilcot GL18 1NH
www.brieryhillllamas.co.uk

Llama experience day in relaxing surroundings, with a private lake and woodland. During your time there you can groom and walk your own llama. Afternoon teas are available.

Photo: Mike White

Nature in Art

Wallsworth Hall, Sandhurst Ln, Twigworth, GL2 9PA
www.natureinart.org.uk

A collection dedicated to nature-inspired fine, decorative, and applied art. Housed in a beautiful Georgian mansion. Wallsworth Hall also offers art classes available, and a cafe serving light refreshments.

Soldiers of Gloucestershire Museum

Back Badge Sq, Gloucester Docks, GL1 2HE
www.soldiersofglos.com

Learn about the lives of Gloucestershire regiment soldiers over the last 300 years. With interactive displays, try on Army uniforms, peer into a trench from World War I, and learn about medals and how soldiers won them throughout history.

Jet Age Museum

Cheltenham Rd East, Gloucester GL2 9QL
www.jetagemuseum.org

Sir Frank Whittle a pioneer of British engineering designed the jet engine and his son Ian is a supporter of the museum. Visit the first jet-powered plane, the first jet fighter, and sit in the cockpit of a 1950s fighter jet or bomber, or a commercial passenger jet, on a guided tour. Enjoy some refreshments at the café.

STOP 8

GLOUCESTERSHIRE ENVIRONS
SUN 2 TO THU 6 AUG (DAY TRIPS)

POSTCODES:

Painswick, Prinknash Abbey, Brockworth, Miserden Park: woodland, picturesque views, rich hunting grounds and stunning country homes.

Painswick village, Gloucestershire

Painswick

On Sunday, 2 August, the royal couple headed to the Cotswold village of Painswick at around 10 in the morning. Beforehand, they were met by Falconer, the mayor in the abbey church yard. The official presented the king with ten fat oxen, for which Henry gave thanks.

Painswick, like many Cotswold towns, also prospered due to the sixteenth-century wool trade. The ancient site of Painswick Beacon offered breathtaking views of Gloucester and its environs. Another point of interest near the beacon was Prinknash Abbey, directly on the route from the city centre. It is rumoured Henry visited there too, though there is no concrete evidence, unlike Painswick. However, it was one of the country residences of the Abbot of Gloucester, which made it likely he visited. A picture-perfect stone mansion, looking out toward Gloucester, it enjoyed spectacular views of the countryside. These days, Prinknash Abbey is a working Benedictine monastery.

Painswick Lodge was an important medieval house in the village in the early 16th century. The former structure was described as having a Great Hall arranged around a courtyard; today, only the west and north ranges remain.

Sources say that a ridge-section of wooded land across the valley from Painswick was long known as The Queen's Wood. (Numerous public footpaths that run through the woods, so you can still walk through them today.)

According to the records, as darkness fell, on their return from Painswick, the group of fifteen riders were greeted at the city gates and escorted through the narrow medieval streets of Gloucester, led by local torch bearers.

Prinknash, Brockworth, Miserden

During the week, Henry and Anne decide to set out in a similar direction for their next day's hunting, heading for the village of Coberley and the park at Miserden, both to the southeast of Gloucester. Once again, before their departure, the royal party were met by the mayor and his entourage. They presented the queen with a purse of gold, for which '*her grace gave loving thanks.*'

Coberley is about nine miles west of Gloucester, the round trip a considerable distance for a hunt. There is speculation that the journey was broken at Brockworth Court, halfway between Gloucester and Coberley. A rumour from the time suggested that Anne stayed at Brockworth while Henry lodged with Catharine of Aragon at nearby Prinknash Abbey in the days before Catharine's court expulsion. Wall paintings at Brockworth from the early sixteenth century depict a Tudor rose next to the religious monogram '*IHC*'. Later investigations showed the stamp had been painted over pomegranates, Catherine's emblem. If Anne's arrival was a snap decision, perhaps orders might have been issued to rapidly cover up the symbols.

The royal party may have also called at Coberley Hall in the village. This was about six miles west of Brockworth Court. Cobberley Hall had been visited by Henry's father and his consort, Elizabeth of York. An opulent and relaxed location, it provided the ideal setting for refreshment and rest and the all-important formation of alliances with the local gentry. The king is then

57

mentioned hunting in Miserden Park, about 3 miles to the south, and although there was no specific mention of Anne, she was likely with him. The royal couple would have been guests of Sir William Kingston, who by a remarkable twist of fate, would serve as Anne's gaoler in his role as Constable of the Tower of London just nine months later.

By 1535, Anne's circle of true friends was shrinking away as her enemies plotted her demise. Kingston, a shadowy but ever-present fellow, began to figure more in Cromwell's activities. Sir William transcribed his conversations with Anne and sent them to Thomas. Kingston's testimony was crucial in her conviction for adultery and high treason. Later, as her jailer, William Kingston accompanied the queen to the scaffold and handed her over to the executioner. Eventually, he would also go on to receive Painswick Lodge, one of the spoils shared after the fall of Cromwell, who had appropriated the property for himself in 1540.

How the rest of the time was spent in Gloucester is unclear.

On Friday, 7 August, Henry gathered outside the abbey in the abbey yard with Anne and the court on the day of departure. They exited to the south of the city, where Southgate Street intersects with Parliament Street, escorted by the same royal processional party that had greeted them, until they arrived at Quedgeley Green, three miles to the south. It must have been quite a spectacle for the locals. According to legend, Anne Boleyn visited Little Thatch, a modest-sized, timber-framed building that still stands in the village. It is still a restaurant and hotel. However, it is unlikely Anne stayed since records confirm the couple were lodged at Leonard Stanley by the evening.

The month-long stay in Gloucestershire meant serving the needs of the king's entourage had the county's highways and byways bustling with the comings and goings of administrators, lords, ladies, and Members of Parliament, clergy, guards, entertainers, jesters, fancy carriages, horses, robbers and vagabonds, and a plethora of tradesmen.

Medieval style pots and tankards

STOP 9
LEONARD STANLEY
FRI 7 AUG 1535

POSTCODE: GL10 3NU

A delightful English village overlooking the Severn Vale.

St Swithun's Church, Leonard Stanley

Leonard Stanley

It was around 16 miles from Gloucester to Berkeley Castle via the Roman road. Gloucester to Leonard Stanley is eleven miles, with a prolonged uphill climb at the end. Continuing onto Berkeley Castle made the total distance from Gloucester Abbey twenty-one miles. This five-mile detour over more difficult terrain, requiring an additional one-night stop in preference to a simpler, easier journey that could have been completed in a day, has historians asking *'why?'*

Leonard Stanley was (and is) a delightful English village overlooking the Severn Vale. It had a priory dedicated to St Leonard, founded around 1131. Three years after the progress, Henry sent an urgent request to the abbot and convent of Gloucester to recall the monks from the priory and grant it to none other than the omnipresent Sir William Kingston. There is also a tenuous link to Cromwell's. Thomas married Elizabeth Wykes, a member of the wealthy Wykes of Chertsey family. In 1535, a man named Nicholas Wykes held the manor of Leonard Stanley. Wykes was married to Elizabeth Poyntz, the aunt of Nicholas Poyntz, owner of Acton Manor in Iron Acton, both of which were on the itinerary for a visit by the king later in the month.

Coaley Peak viewpoint over the Severn Vale

STOP 10
BERKELEY CASTLE
SAT 8 AUG 1535

POSTCODE: GL13 9BQ

The history played out within Berkeley Castle's walls make it one of the most remarkable buildings in Britain.

Berkeley Castle, Gloucestershire

Berkeley Castle

It was Henry and Anne's first and last visit to Berkeley, but they were clearly determined to enjoy its pleasant charms, as provision had been made in the geists for them to stay for the entire week.

Thomas Cromwell was still close to the king's side, busy overseeing the *'visits'* already being made to several monastic houses from the profusion of letters recorded in Letters and Papers that continue throughout the progress.

Less imposing than other Norman fortresses such as Ludlow or Dover, Berkeley didn't dominate the buildings around it.

The less political Berkeley family had concentrated on creating a residential rather than defensive development. Screened by the church and trees, it is more clearly viewed from the south, across the marshy meadows beside the banks of the Avon River.

Built in the 11th and developed in the 12th and 14th centuries on a typical Norman motte and bailey design, it is also highly distinctive because of the materials used in its construction, local pink, grey, and yellow Severn sandstone, with roofs primarily fashioned in Cotswold stone, slate, or lead.

Despite its decorative exterior, barbaric acts still occurred in the castle. It still can't shake the stigma of royal murder since Edward II supposedly died in gruesome and sadistic circumstances on 21 September 1327, at the hands of his captors within the keep's walls, his screams allegedly heard miles away. Others, such William Melton, Archbishop of York, said he had escaped from Berkeley Castle and travelled to Corfe Castle, then onto Ireland, then Avignon to visit the pope, Germany, and finally settling in an Italian hermitage, calling himself *'William the Welshman'* when he met his son Edward III. (Something to ponder on your travels.)

Engraving of King Edward III

The interiors of Berkeley remained largely unchanged from the sixteenth century until the 1920s when the 8th Earl modernised the building. The good news is the rooms used by Henry and Anne still exist in the *'great suite'*. Although structural changes have occurred over time, and some of the more interesting parts of the castle are now off-limits, the tone of the interior design has been little altered in the intervening centuries. Most of the furniture dates before the 1660s.

Although the Berkeley family archives are extensive, few records survive from the sixty-year period when the castle was in Crown hands, leaving historians to speculate on what happened during Henry and Anne's six-day stay. Evenings would probably be spent gambling, conversing, listening to music, and dancing and the days filled with hunting and hawking in the beautiful south Gloucestershire landscape.

Sir William Paulet's household accounts confirm the date they left—Saturday, 14 August, when the court travelled to Thornbury, another beautiful castle.

Sir William Paulet

Visiting

The castle is not open all year round, so for opening times, dates, and other visitor information, please visit the website:

- www.berkeley-castle.com

Berkeley attractions

Photo: Else Rolle

Dr Jenner's House, Museum and Garden

Church Lane, Berkeley GL13 9BN
www.jennermuseum.com

Edward Jenner, born in 1749, spent much of his early life exploring the fields and hedgerows that surrounded the Gloucestershire town of Berkeley. Jenner, then 23, returned to Berkeley with a renewed desire to discover the secrets of the natural world after training as a surgeon in London. Early experiments included medicine, horticulture, and the natural world. Jenner was awarded a Royal Society Fellowship for a paper on the nesting habits of cuckoos. In 1796, he performed the world's first controlled smallpox vaccination. Soon after, he set up a free vaccination clinic in the Temple of Vaccinia, a rustic hut in his tranquil garden.

STOP 11
THORNBURY
FRI 14 AUG 1535

POSTCODE: BS35 1HH

Beautiful 16th-century building, which was once owned by Henry. Now a hotel open to the public, surrounded by Tudor Walled Gardens.

Thornbury Castle, Gloucestershire

Thornbury Castle

The distance between Berkeley Castle and Thornbury Castle is only seven miles. The Roman road that leads to Bristol is straight and level. Given the size of a royal procession and the proximity of the two castles, it is feasible that both were used for lodging at the same time. However, some historians have indicated evidence that the king was staying away from court, hunting in the Welsh Marches, and dealing with correspondence with Cromwell in Bewdley. Another point to ponder on your journey.

Thornbury, located on the outskirts of the Cotswolds in South Gloucestershire, and the former Tudor castle is now a hotel open to the public. Jasper Tudor, Henry VII's uncle, lived there until he died in 1495. It fell into Crown hands when Henry had his distant cousin, Edward Stafford, 3rd Duke of Buckingham, executed for treason. Had the duke completed his bold design for the property, it would have been one of the most magnificent construction projects of the time, comparable only to Wolsey's Hampton Court Palace. It was not intended to be a fortress but rather a majestic and comfortable family home—though it could have been defended if necessary.

Henry took the castle for himself and stayed at Thornbury with Anne from 14 August 1535 until their departure for Acton Court on 22 August.

Here, the progress deviated from the planned *'geists'*. Bristol was supposed to be the tour's farthest outpost from the start, and from there, the journey would begin the long journey home. But, unfortunately, the *'Western Capital of England'* was out of bounds in August 1535, a visitation of the plague beating the monarch to the city. So instead, an envoy of representatives travelled out to see the king, bearing the obligatory gifts.

Visiting

For more information about visiting the hotel and the range of services available for guests, visit the website:

- www.thornburycastle.co.uk

A dessert at Thornbury Castle

STOP 12
IRON ACTON
FRI 21 AUG 1535

POSTCODE: BS37 9TL (ACTON COURT)

The court offers a rare example of 16th-century royal state apartments and decor, which is the finest of its kind in England

Acton Court, now a private home, Gloucestershire

Acton Court

Thornbury Castle to Acton Court was a six-mile trip.

The host, Sir Nicholas Poyntz, a young twenty-three-year-old knighted during the visit, was married to Joan, daughter of Thomas Berkeley, 5th Baron Berkeley. According to legend, Poyntz had spent the previous nine months constructing a new east wing in preparation for the August visit. Instead, the royal entourage arrived on the 21st, two days later than originally planned.

Sir Nicholas Poyntz (after Hans Holbein)

Sir Nicholas Poyntz was a royal favourite and zealous Reformer, earning his knighthood during the stay. On the outskirts of Iron Acton, Acton Court had an entire new wing added to impress his royal visitors. Hurriedly built to meet the deadline for the visit, it lacked proper foundations. Despite the hurried timescale, Poyntz chose decor fit for a king and queen, furnishing the new rooms with high-end items like Venetian glass, modelling them in the style of two royal palaces, Hampton Court and Whitehall.

The magnificent new east wing was added to the existing moated house. The rectangular, two-story addition, built on the site of the medieval kitchens, contained three grand state apartments on the first floor, each with a fireplace and an adjacent garderobe (en suite) and decorated in the latest Renaissance style.

One of the new rooms, the privy chamber, was to be guarded by the king's gentlemen ushers and was only accessible to the dedicated staff whose job it was to attend to Henry around the clock, or to those specifically invited by the king. According to the Eltham Ordinance of 1526, another of Henry's many palaces, there were six gentlemen, two ushers, four grooms, a barber, and a page all reporting to the Groom of the Stool, Sir Henry Norris.

The royal couple could also enjoy the gardens from this wing via a covered gallery that spanned the moat.

Henry would have made the most of the hunting opportunities available in Acton's two deer parks. The arrangement of the rooms on the lower floor is unclear, and Poyntz remodelled the building some years later, leaving historians to suppose where Anne may have stayed during the progress.

As time passed, the royal tour began to take on a more evangelical tone. The next stop, six miles away, at Little Sodbury Manor, was the home of Sir John Walsh.

Sir John and Lady Anne Walsh were Nicolas Poyntz's maternal uncle and aunt, and all of them were connected to a high-profile political and religious friend, William Tyndale, the former tutor of Walsh's sons. At the time of the progress, Tynedale was under investigation for illegally translating the Bible into English from Latin.

Since the seventh century, attacks on bible-transcribers sent a strong signal that the English church wished to keep all scripture knowledge to itself hidden behind the archaic Latin language. The clergy feared that if the people knew what was written in the bible, they would demand more freedom. Worse, they might wonder why anyone needed church authority when they could communicate with Jesus directly—through their own English-language copy of the work.

Tyndale had left England eleven years earlier, in 1524, during Wolsey's vice-like tenure, bound for Germany, fleeing the fall-out from criticising Henry's divorce from Catherine. Tyndale's criticism was so vehement that the king asked the Holy Roman Emperor, Charles V to have him arrested and deported to England. He had not returned home in eleven years, living as a wanted man. He had been in hiding for nine months in Antwerp, until the spring of 1535, under the protection of Thomas Poyntz, a cousin from the Poyntz family's Essex line.

The Bishop of London, John Stokesley, was most likely behind covert efforts to apprehend Tyndale. Poyntz went about his business on the continent, travelling the Easter Fair, and while he was gone, Tyndale was lured into the confidence of, and later betrayed by, an Englishman, Harry Philips. On May 21, 1535, Tyndale was arrested.

The *'royal couple'* arrived at Acton three months after Tyndale's imprisonment, who was still critical about their marriage.

On 25 August 1535, Thomas Poyntz of Antwerp wrote a letter to his brother John in England pleading with him to ask the English government for more assistance for Tyndale.

He informed his brother that Cromwell's letters written on behalf of the king had been intercepted somewhere along the line. Cromwell continued to work on Tyndale's behalf for the next year or so, but in early October 1536, he was dragged from his cell before being throttled to death then burned at the stake in Vilvoorde, near modern-day Brussels. His final words were, 'Lord, open the King of England's eyes.'

Within four years, at the king's request, four English translations of the bible were published in England, including Henry's official *'Great Bible'*. Tyndale's work served as the foundation for all of them.

For Anne, her next host, Walsh, was to be the one whose testimony would be crucial in hastening her own death.

Visiting

Visiting today: Acton Court is seldom open to the public, only accessible on occasional days throughout the year. Check the website:

- www.actoncourt.com

STOP 13
LITTLE SODBURY
MON 24 AUG 1535

POSTCODE: BS37 6QB (VILLAGE)

Private 15th-century manor house in picturesque Little Sodbury, a 'Thankful Village' that lost no men in WWI.

St. Adelines Church, Little Sodbury, Gloucestershire

Little Sodbury Manor

The Walshes, like their nephew, supported reform and thus received the honour of a royal visit. However, while Tynedale worked for the family, he met and debated religious matters with churchmen from neighbouring monastic houses, and he also began preaching in the local villages. This got him in trouble with the authorities.

William Tynedale

As well as publishing his first copy of the translated bible in 1526, Tyndale went on to write other important and controversial works that drew Anne's attention, most notably the *'Obedience of a Christian Man'*, which was published in 1528, while William was in exile on the continent. Soon after it was purchased, Anne purchased a copy and highlighted passages of interest to show Henry.

Tyndale set out to demonstrate that God required Henry's subjects to obey him, and if they did not, they were not only disobeying their prince but also God. It goes without saying that Tyndale's message resonated with Henry. However, a later publication would invite Henry's wrath and would cost Tynedale his life.

In 1530, he decided to write *'The Practyse of Prelates'*, which argued that Henry's planned divorce was unscriptural. He even dared to speak favourably of Katharine of Aragon. Henry became enraged and demanded his arrest and extradition.

Nonetheless, over the next few years, Anne and Cromwell worked quietly to smooth things over. Anne even owned a copy of Tyndale's New Testament's banned revised edition. Perhaps Tyndale's predicament was a talking point at Tyndale's former home in Little Sodbury. Anne had no idea that she would be facing the executioner months before the man she was attempting to save.

Little Sodbury Manor, now a private residence, was largely constructed in the mid-fifteenth century, incorporating parts of an earlier timber-framed house, and was remodelled by Sir John Walsh between 1510 and 1520.

Visiting

Little Sodbury is a private home and does not allow viewings. However, the nearby village is worth visiting.

Photo: Steve Knight

Aerospace Bristol

Hayes Way Filton, Patchway BS34 5BZ
www.aerospacebristol.org

From the first aeroplanes to space technology and the supersonic Concorde, take an immersive, hands-on journey through more than a century of astounding aviation achievements.

Dyrham Park

Dyrham, Near Bath, SN14 8ER
www.nationaltrust.org.uk

William Blathwayt devised Dyrham Park in the 17th century. Dyrham was one of the most notable stately homes of the period. The 270-acre ancient parkland is home to magnificent trees, breathtaking views, and plenty of space for young (and older!) explorers to roam. The stunning surrounding gardens include magnificent borders, idyllic ponds, and a wildflower orchard.

Chippenham Museum

10 Market Place, Chippenham SN15 3HF
www.chippenham.gov.uk/chippenham-museum

Housed in an 18th century townhouse, the museum tells the fascinating storey of this historic market town from its prehistoric origins to the present day. Discover the town's history through its connections to the river, road, and rail, as well as its surprising connections to Alfred the Great and Isambard Kingdom Brunel.

Bowood House and Gardens

Old Rd, Derry Hill, Chippenham SN11 0LZ
www.bowood.org

Discover the rich and fascinating history of the house and the Lansdowne family, which is set within 100 acres of beautifully landscaped 'Capability' Brown Parkland. The Italian-inspired terrace garden, private walled gardens, and herbaceous border surround the Georgian house, all of which are vibrantly coloured throughout the seasons. Younger visitors will enjoy the adventure playground and life-size pirate ship.

71

STOP 14
BROMHAM
THU 27 AUG 1535

> **POSTCODE: SN15 2PR (VILLAGE)**

Nothing remains of this once magnificent house, large enough to house 700 people.

The Palace of Whitehall, comparable to Bromham House in scale.

Bromham House

Next, the royal party travelled the 12 miles from Little Sodbury to Bromham House, the home of Anne's Vice-Chamberlain, Sir Edward Baynton, another reformer and a long-time favourite of Henry. Supporter and possible favourite of Catherine of Aragon, the relationship was not as friendly for Anne. A few months later, Bayntun was one of those who stuck the knife into the new queen when she faced her string of adultery accusations, trying to secure confessions from the men.

> 'Only the wretched Mark Smeaton would confess against the Queen, although I have no doubt the others were as fully culpable as ever was he.'

Sir Edward Bayntun's estate was located about a mile northeast of Bromham village. Bromham House was a grand mansion, reportedly big enough to house seven hundred people and said to be nearly as large as the Palace of Whitehall, decorated with stone carvings and very richly furnished. Baynton entertained his sovereigns and the court for a week at this magnificent residence.

Visiting

Very little of the residence remains, except for the stone gatehouse, Spye Arch, which survived two great fires at the Bayntun properties.

The park's grounds are not open to the public, but the gatehouse, Spye Arch Lodge, which used to serve Bromham House, can be seen from the road.

It is off the A342 Devizes Road, opposite The George Inn. Be warned, there is no parking.

If you do make the journey, the arms of Henry VIII can be seen beneath the window.

Spye House before it was destroyed by fire

STOP 15
BURBAGE
THU 3 SEPT 1535

POSTCODE: SN8 3DP (VILLAGE)

The village that was home to the legendary Wolfhall, seat of the Seymour family, and the residence of future Queen Jane.

St Mary's Church, Burbage by Asteuartw

Wolfhall

Wiltshire was the wealthiest and most powerful county in the country in 1535, at the epicentre of the political and religious upheaval. The county had far more Members of Parliament than any other in the country, nearly double that of second-placed Dorset. Within a year, it would provide the next queen of England through a political marriage and give legitimacy to a new government faction.
Spawned by Wolsey, the Boleyn faction now lacked numbers. Moreover, the group had always been reliant on French sponsorship, which was evaporating—quickly. In the longer term, even headstrong Henry would seek advice from his advisors. Soon, the Seymour-Cromwell faction would rule his kingdom.

Jane Seymour

Wolfhall, on the outskirts of Savernake Forest, was the Wiltshire home of Sir John Seymour, whose eldest daughter Jane would become Henry's third wife in less than nine months.

Unfortunately, this was not the *'bolt of lightning'* moment of true love. Although Henry might have met Jane at this point, it would not be much later, until 10 February 1536, at least that ambassador Chapuys informed Charles V that Henry was paying particular attention to Jane.

The progress was running behind again, but only by one day. The royal party arrived on Friday, 3 September and stayed for around a week.

Several important documents relating to the appointment of three new reformist bishops—Edward Fox, Hugh Latimer, and John Hilsey—were signed on September 7 at Wolfhall in preparation for their consecration later on the tour at Winchester around 19 September.

The house where the royal progress stayed has long since vanished, and its exact location is unknown, but it is believed that some remnants of the original Wolfhall are built into the current farm buildings.

Visiting

Nothing of the hall the progress visited remains, but stained glass depicting Jane Seymour's phoenix badge, the Tudor rose, and the Prince of Wales feathers originally installed at Wolfhall were moved to St Mary's church (SN8 3PE) after the house was destroyed. The church also houses Sir John Seymour's impressive tomb, a man who undoubtedly played a role in Anne's fall from grace.

The modern hall's location is inaccessible, but it can be seen from the road at any reasonable hour.

STOP 16
THRUXTON
WED 9 SEP 1535

POSTCODE: SP11 8NL (VILLAGE)

A Hampshire village with a manor house, thatched cottages, village green and a 15th-century pub. The original hall is gone.

St-Peter-And-St-Paul's Church, Thruxton by TrishSteel

Thomas Lisle's House

Henry and Anne, accompanied by Thomas Cromwell, stayed at courtier Thomas Lisle's house in Thruxton. Thomas had begun his career in the household of his distant cousin, childless Sir John Lisle. The Lisles were prominent members of Hampshire's landed gentry. To preserve the family name, John married Lisle to his niece and heir, Mary Kingston. Thomas became Henry's Esquire of the Body—a personal attendant on the king and thus a trustworthy host on the progress. Many holders of the role progressed onto highly influential positions later.

Visiting

Nothing remains of the house Henry and Anne visited, although the Lisle family tombs are in Thruxton's St Peter and St Paul's village church (SP11 8NL), dating from the thirteenth century.

Website:

- explorechurches.org/church/st-peter-st-paul-thruxton

Bromham attractions

Photo: Andrew Bone

Atwell-Wilson Motor Museum

Stockley Rd, Calne SN11 0NF
www.atwellwilson.org.uk

A small, inviting museum in the heart of Wiltshire. The majority of the exhibits are cars from the 1920s and later, as well as a collection of motorcycles, mopeds, and push bikes, along with motoring memorabilia and a recreated 1930s-style garage complete with cars.

Lacock Abbey

Lacock Abbey High St, Lacock SN15 2LG
www.nationaltrust.org.uk

The abbey, set in its own woodland in the heart of the village, is a whimsical country house of multiple architectural styles built on the foundations of a former nunnery. Visitors can indulge themselves in the ambience of the mediaeval rooms and cloister court, which evokes the Aabbey's monastic past.

The museum honours former Lacock resident William Henry Fox Talbot, who is best known for his accomplishments in the invention of photography.

Wiltshire Museum

41 Long St, Devizes SN10 1NS
www.wiltshiremuseum.org.uk

The best Bronze Age archaeology collection in the United Kingdom. Explore the galleries, see the outstanding collections, and learn more about Wiltshire's and its people's rich history over the last 6,000 years. Learn about the people who built and used the world-famous Stonehenge and Avebury monuments. Unusual gold and amber objects date back over 4,000 years to the Bronze Age, a time of shamans and priests, learning, and culture throughout Europe. Later periods, such as the Iron Age, Romans, and Saxons, are also discussed, as is the history of Devizes and the surrounding area.

Photo Roy W

Wadworth Brewery

41-45 Northgate Street, Devizes SN10 1JW
www.wadworth.co.uk

Discover the history and heritage of Wadworth Brewery while sampling the delights of their famous ales. This educational experience, which includes a 'Brewseum' of Wadworth memorabilia, interactive displays showcasing traditional brewing methods, a sample bar, and a fully stocked gift shop, allows visitors to understand all aspects of this busy, working brewery, from 1875 to the present day.

Cherhill White Horse and Monument

Near Calne SN11 8XY
www.nationaltrust.org.uk

The iconic Cherhill White Horse, one of only eight chalk white horses in Wiltshire, can be seen for miles around. It is the second oldest in Wiltshire, built in 1780 under the supervision of Dr Christopher Alsop of Calne with a megaphone, who gave instructions to a team of workers on the hillside. The horse's outline had faded with time, and in 2002 it needed to be re-cut. 160 tonnes of fresh chalk were packed onto the horse, held in place by wooden boarding. It is maintained by the Cherhill White Horse Restoration Group, with the assistance of the local scout group, by weeding and re-chalking every two years.

Caen Hill Locks

Car Park 1, The Locks, Devizes SN10 1PR
canalrivertrust.org.uk

The Kennet and Avon Canal contains some outstanding examples of waterway engineering. The 16 locks that comprise the flight's steepest section at Caen Hill are not only a designated ancient monument, but also an olympic-sized challenge that every boater must complete. This "wonder of the waterway" is a must-see for canal boaters. With a total of 29 locks, it is one of the country's longest continuous flight of locks. Over a two-mile stretch, the water level rises by an astounding 237 feet.

Wilton Windmill

Wilton Hill, Wilton, Marlborough SN8 3SW
www.wiltonwindmill.co.uk

Wilton Windmill, located high above the village of Wilton, is Wessex's only working windmill and continues to produce wholemeal, stone-ground flour.

The windmill building, located at the eastern end of Pewsey Vale, is open for guided tours and contains a granary, cafe, and shop. In the heart of the North Wessex Downs, you'll find a tranquil and stunning landscape of rolling chalk downland, forests, woods, and dales.

Photo: Chris Allen

Crofton Beam Engines

Crofton Pumping Station, Marlborough SN8 3DW
www.croftonbeamengines.org

Step into the UKs industrial and social history and turn back the clock to a time when steam was king. The station was constructed in 1807-9 to provide water to the highest point of the Kennet & Avon Canal, which connects London and Bristol. It is a rare survivor of the technology that allowed British engineers to drain mines and supply water to towns and cities all over the world.

STOP 17
HURSTBOURNE PRIORS
SAT 12 SEP 1535

POSTCODE: RG28 7RN

Little remains of the stunning priory and the exceptional hunting grounds.

St Andrews Church, Hurstbourne Priors by Mike Cattell

Hurstbourne Priors Manor

The monks of Winchester, specifically the Priory of St Swithun, owned the priory when the royal party swept into Hurstbourne Park in the early autumn of 1535. This is another venue shrouded in mystery. A map from 1575 suggested a manor house built over the River Bourne and an enclosed deer park to the northwest. Given the brevity of the visit, it is unlikely the couple hunted there. The rest of the medieval layout and appearance is unknown. The manor house was replaced twice, with the current building constructed in the late Victorian era. The Earls of Portsmouth currently reside on the estate, the entirety of which is inaccessible to the public.

Visiting

This stop has been included to complete the route, but there is nothing special to recommend a visit, apart from not missing out something on the geist.

Hurstbourne Priors attractions

Photo: Simon Burchill

Whitchurch Silk Mill

28 Winchester St, Whitchurch RG28 7AL
www.whitchurchsilkmill.org.uk

Whitchurch Silk Mill is a 19th-century water mill that continues to weave English silk fabrics with 19th-century machinery. Whitchurch Silk Mill has something for everyone, whether you're a machine enthusiast, a fan of silk fabrics, a child learning about the Victorians, or just looking for a fun day out. This is a great day out for all ages, with the original mill wheel and Victorian machinery, fabulous fabrics on the looms, a shop to indulge in silk products from the mill, and a peaceful setting by the River Test, with tearoom for lunch and refreshments.

Bombay Sapphire Distillery

Laverstoke Mill, London Rd, Whitchurch RG28 7NR
www.bombaysapphire.com

Explore the distillery with a guide to learn about the ten exotic botanicals that are infused into every drop of Bombay Sapphire Gin in the glasshouses. Enjoy the Botanical Dry Room, a sensory experience that will help you discover your flavour preferences. Discover the rare vapour infusion distillation process that distinguishes Bombay Sapphire gin before your host departs to enjoy a cocktail based on your flavour preferences.

Highclere Castle

Highclere Park, Highclere RG20 9RN
www.highclerecastle.co.uk

Highclere Castle is best known as the fictional home of the Crawley family and their servants in the TV show Downton Abbey. In reality, it has been the Earls of Carnarvon's family seat since 1679. The family was involved in the establishment of Canada, the discovery of King Tutankhamun's tomb in Egypt, scandalous affairs, and shady court cases. Highclere Castle has hosted royalty, politicians, famous writers, and film stars.

STOP 18
WINCHESTER
SAT 12 SEPT 1535

> **POSTCODE: SO23 9LS (WINCHESTER)**

An unspoilt cathedral city beside the rolling South Downs National Park, England's ancient capital and former seat of Alfred the Great.

Winchester Cathedral, Hampshire

83

Wolvesey Palace

The start of a long stay until 30 September, with a short tour to Bishop's Waltham. Despite its majestic rolling countryside and ancient woodlands, Anglo-Saxon England's capital has long been associated with kings and queens. The royal couple is thought to have stayed at Wolvesey Palace, the bishop's palace, since the royal apartments at the castle had been destroyed by fire in 1302. The itinerary for the stay was thrown out of the window. The original plan was for the royal couple to stay in Winchester for four or five days before moving the 7 miles to Bishop's Waltham; however, the royal couple were so taken with the sport on offer in the area, particularly the hawking, that they extended their stay to at least two weeks

The most important aspect of the visit was the appointment of three reforming bishops in September 1535, the backdrop to the culmination of the progress.

The ceremony was performed in the presence of the king and Anne by Thomas Cranmer, Archbishop of Canterbury.

Wolvesey Place, Winchester

Wolvesey Palace was a lavish palace built largely in the twelfth century by the powerful Bishop Henry of Blois, brother of King Stephen and grandson of William the Conqueror. Subsequent owners extended and refurbished it extensively over the centuries. However, the palace was used primarily for state occasions rather than as a permanent residence beginning in the early fourteenth century.

It is possible the royal guests were accommodated in rooms in the west range, which served as the principal residence and private apartments of the Bishop of Winchester, who was Stephen Gardiner at the time of Anne's visit. It is still the residence to this day.

Today, all that remains of the palace that Anne would have known are ruins and a fifteenth-century chapel incorporated into a baroque palace built in the seventeenth century on the same site.

The ruins are open to the public.

At Winchester, Anne was entertained by a handsome Flemish musician, Mark Smeaton, known for his singing and dancing abilities in Henry's court, who later transferred to the queen's court. Multi-talented, in addition to singing and dancing, he could also play the lute, viol, virginals, and organ. Anne requested his presence during the long stay.

Mark Smeaton's exact birth date is unknown, but he was believed to be around 23 or 24 years old when he died the following year. While little is known about Smeaton's life, it is assumed that he was the son of a carpenter and a seamstress. His surname was common in the Flemish area.

He first joined Thomas Wolsey's choir, but following the cardinal's demise, Smeaton was transferred from the cardinal's service to Henry's Chapel Royal, where his musical ability caught the queen's attention. In 1532, he was named a Groom of the Privy Chamber after establishing himself as a court musician. Of low social standing, he was never destined to be part of the queen's close circle of friends, made up of her favourite ladies-in-waiting and most loyal courtiers. Anne herself chastised him for assuming she would address him in the same way she would an aristocrat.

Winchester attractions

The Great Hall

Castle Avenue, Winchester SO23 8UJ
www.hants.gov.uk

The Great Hall, described as 'one of the finest surviving aisled halls of the 13th century,' houses the most famous symbol of mediaeval mythology, King Arthur's Round Table, and is all that remains of Winchester Castle. This is one of the finest surviving examples of a 13th century aisled hall and is an addition to William the Conqueror's original Winchester Castle. Discover the history and uncover the battles, secrets, and terrorism and treason trials that have taken place here. Also, see the legendary Round Table of Arthur, which has dominated Winchester's ancient Great Hall for centuries.

Winchester Cathedral

9 The Close, Winchester, SO23 9LS
www.winchester-cathedral.org.uk

The Cathedral Church of the Holy Trinity, Saint Peter, Saint Paul, and Saint Swithun, usually known as Winchester Cathedral, is amongst the largest of its kind in Northern Europe. The current cathedral was built between 1079 and 1532 and is dedicated to Saint Swithun of Winchester. It has a Perpendicular Gothic nave, and Norman transepts and tower. It is the world's longest mediaeval cathedral, surpassing only St Peter's Basilica in Rome, Our Lady of Peace Basilica in Yamoussoukro, Ivory Coast, Liverpool Anglican Cathedral, the Cathedral of St John the Divine in New York City, and Basilica of Our Lady in Aparecida. It is the sixth-largest cathedral in the UK, behind Liverpool, St Paul's, York, Westminster Catholic and Lincoln.

Jane Austen's House

Winchester Rd, Chawton, Alton GU34 1SD
janeaustens.house

Jane Austen revised, wrote, and published all six of her beloved novels in this charming Hampshire cottage. Today, you can travel back in time to 1816 and walk in Jane's shoes, visiting the rooms where she wrote her books and created her timeless characters, exploring her home, objects that belonged to her, and wandering in the pretty cottage garden.

STOP 19
BISHOP'S WALTHAM
SAT 26 SEPT 1535 (OVERNIGHT TOUR)

POSTCODE: SO32 1DH (PALACE)

A vibrant and historic market town set in the glorious Hampshire countryside. The bishop's residence now lies in ruin.

Bishop's Waltham Palace by Gerd Eichmann, Hampshire

Bishop's Waltham Palace

It appears that Henry and Anne joined the wider court at Bishop's Waltham at some point, probably after the consecration of the three bishops in Winchester, before returning to Winchester again before the court's removal southwards to Southampton.

Bishop's Waltham Palace was a substantial property in the sixteenth century, having been owned by the bishops of Winchester since the twelfth century. It was thought to be big enough to house the whole court.

The formidable Stephen Gardiner, who was made Bishop of Winchester in 1532, was its owner at the time of the progress and must have had the job of formally entertaining his royal guests while they lodged in Winchester and Waltham.

Gardiner, like Sir William Paulet, owner of Basing House, was a Tudor survivor.

Waltham Palace was demolished during the Civil War. Defended at first by the royalists, it was ruined when it was captured by Parliamentarian forces, and the valuable materials were stripped to be used elsewhere.

Visiting

The palace ruins leave enough for the visitor to imagine the former grandeur of the building. The ruins are open for part of the year, but the nearby town of the same name is worth visiting.

There is a small car park on-site, and admission is free.

Bishop's Waltham High Street, Hampshire

STOP 20
SOUTHAMPTON
WED 30 SEPT 1535

POSTCODE: SO14 2AD (MERCHANT'S HOUSE)

The medieval town walls and former entrance—the Bargate – still stand today in this busy modern port.

Tudor Merchant's Town House, Bugle Street, Southampton

Southampton Castle or Merchant House

Regrettably, the records are patchy for the Southampton visit, though it is suspected the couple stayed at either Southampton Castle or the Tudor House Museum, now on Bugle Street. It was not planned on the original geists.

Since Roman times, Southampton had been a major trading port, the third-largest in England. Up to the sixteenth century, it was used for importing French wine, luxuries such as spices, perfumes, and silk, and shipments of alum and woad used in dyeing wool, the town's main export. Well-to-do merchants moved into the High Street, described as *'one of the fairest in all England for timber buildings.'* Skilled tradesmen also flocked to the area. However, by 1535, the town had begun to decline. Trade was dwindling, and Cromwell and the townsfolk debated the town's debts and who should foot the bill to repair the city walls.

The townspeople complained about dwindling trade in 1533, just two years before the royal visit, and by 1535, Cromwell was being asked to clear Southampton's debts in exchange for the people of town repairing the city walls. However, the matter was not resolved. The buildings began to crumble, and weeds and climbing plants took root in gaps in the stone.

Southampton's castle was owned directly by the king, and he had a constable who oversaw it daily, which has earmarked it to historians as a likely place for the royal couple to reside. Also, Henry had stayed there before.

However, there is a local tale that another building, which still stands today in all its Tudor glory on modern-day Bugle Street, was used. A sizable townhouse, it reflects the wealth and power of its sixteenth-century owner, Sir Richard Lyster (1480–1553), husband of property's heiress, Isabel Dawtrey. Richard was also Henry's Lord Chief Justice, putting him in a position to help the king with his Great Matter in 1533. He also had a hand in Sir Thomas More's trial earlier in the year. Given his obvious support for the Boleyn match, it's easy to see why Sir Richard was so honoured.

Visiting

The Tudor Merchant's house is on Bugle Street. Visit the website for more details:

- www.tudorhouseandgarden.com

Also take a look at another Tudor house in the area, on neighbouring French Street. (SO14 2AT)

Southampton attractions

Photo: Peter Langsdale

Solent Sky Museum

Albert Rd South, Southampton SO14 3FR
www.solentskymuseum.org

Between 1910 and 1960, Hampshire and the Solent region were the world's centre for aviation research and development. More than 26 aircraft manufacturers established themselves in this area, producing everything from biplanes to spacecraft, including the legendary Spitfire. Solent Sky tells the amazing story of aviation in the region through more than 20 vintage aircraft.

Beaulieu National Motor Museum

John Montagu Bldg, Beaulieu SO42 7ZN
www.beaulieu.co.uk

The world-museum has one of the world's finest collections of cars, motorcycles, and motoring memorabilia, ranging from the earliest motor carriages to classic family saloons. Plus if you ever wondered what happened to the cars that were battered, modified, and generally ruined by the BBC's Top Gear team, you'll find them in a special exhibition. There are also famous cars from film and screen on display, from Mr Bean, to Dr Who.

For history buffs, Palace House, once the mediaeval Beaulieu Abbey's gatehouse, has been the Montagu family home since 1538. The 800-year-old Abbey was founded in the 13th century by King John and was destroyed on King Henry VIII's orders. The now tranquil abbey is a conserved ruin thanks to the efforts of the Montagu family ancestors. It is surrounded by relaxing gardens.

Exbury Gardens and Steam Railway

Summer Lane, Exbury, Hampshire SO45 1AZ
www.exbury.co.uk

Exbury Gardens & Steam Railway, which has been in the works for over a century, is a spectacular collection of landscaped woodland, herbaceous, contemporary, and formal gardens in a one-of-a-kind riverside location. Exbury also has a narrow-gauge steam railway that runs through the gardens, as well as a playground and a restaurant.

STOP 21
PORTCHESTER
SUN 4 OCT 1535

> **POSTCODE: PO16 9QW (CASTLE)**

One of the best-preserved Roman forts. Built in the 3rd century, it's the only Roman stronghold in northern Europe whose walls still stand.

Portchester Castle, Portsmouth, Hampshire

Portchester Castle

On arrival at the castle, Henry and Anne most likely stayed at the King's Lodgings. Lord Lisle wrote to Sir Richard Graynfeld, telling him, *'The king intends going to Portchester in your ship on Monday [the 4th].'* However, the accommodation was cramped and outdated, and thus the stay was short.

On the Hampshire coastline, Portchester was one of a string of Roman defensive forts built around AD 280 by the Romans, stretching around the south and eastern shores to Branchester in Norfolk. It was then occupied by the Saxons.

The eroded remains of the once-appealing porch leading up to the Great Hall, as well as the finely moulded, towering windows that let light into it and the king's privy chamber, tell of stately apartments that once occupied the inner bailey's south-west corner, adjacent to the keep.

Henry's father initiated a programme to build warships for an English navy. As a result, there were five royal warships by the time Henry VII died. Two of them were brand-new four-masted battleships, far larger than the average English merchant ship. At the end of Henry's reign, the navy had grown to more than 40 ships.

When most people think of the Tudor navy, they think of Elizabeth I defeating the Spanish Armada—or the sinking of Henry's flagship, the Mary Rose. However, England's 16th-century maritime fighting force has far greater historical significance than these two landmark events.

Sea battles were uncommon in the medieval period. Mostly, any action fought close to shore was a coastal raid or estuary skirmish. However, naval warfare changed dramatically during the 16th century, with the introduction of heavy artillery making a significant difference in at-sea combat.

Henry, dubbed the *'father of the Royal Navy'* by many, was the first king to make a concerted effort to transform England into a sea power to be reckoned with, recognising that command of the sea was critical to any successful military campaign.

Henry always intended to fight the French, and he knew that getting his fleet to sea before the enemy would give him a huge advantage. Rather than assembling one from scratch for each campaign, having a standing navy would serve this purpose best.

In 1512 and 1513, Henry's navy fought off the coast of Brittany, and in 1522 and 1523, it raided the French coast. During the 1520s and 1530s, it also conducted summer and winter patrols against pirates. Meanwhile, Henry's break with Rome in 1534 put England in grave danger of an invasion sanctioned by the Pope. The fleet was mobilised during an invasion scare in 1539, though it saw no action.

Ships were mostly built in small yards along the Thames and the Medway. A few were created at Woolwich. Portsmouth and Southampton had shipyards where, at the start of Henry's reign, the infamous Mary Rose and the ship with Catherine of Aragon's emblem, the Peter Pomegranate, among other vessels were built. These differed from their forefathers in that many were larger, and they were customised warships with gun decks. Elizabeth was more concerned with pirates and excelled at building nimble galleons of varying sizes, suitable for both oceanic travel and confronting Spain in the New World.

The Tudor navy was largely responsible for creating the enduring image of England as a great maritime power and successfully defending England from foreign invasion.

During this period, English mariners also gained the confidence to embark on long-distance voyages and the necessary navigational skills.

The Tudors left behind a highly developed infrastructure and a culture of success that the Stuart dynasty squandered. The establishment of the Royal Navy, encouraging shipbuilding, and establishing dockyards was an important part of Henry's legacy.

Salisbury, the next stop, was 40 miles and three to four days' travel away. The couple's arrival is mentioned on 9 October. The interim itinerary is unclear.

Portsmouth attractions

The Mary Rose

Main Road Portsmouth Naval Base PO1 3PY
www.maryrose.org

Henry VIII ordered the Mary Rose to be built on ascending to the throne in 1509. Construction began in 1510, and she was finally launched in 1511. The Mary Rose would later fight in two wars, one against France and one against Scotland. Part of the Portsmouth Historic Dockyard complex, home to Nelson's HMS Victory and HMS Warrior, Britain's first iron-hulled, armoured battleship.

(The rest of the Portsmouth Docks area is worth exploring, including HMS Victory and the boat tours. Over the water, the submarine museum at Gosport has a lot to offer.)

The Mary Rose, photo by Geni

STOP 22
SALISBURY
FRI 9 OCT 1535

POSTCODE: SP1 2QB (CHURCH HOUSE)

Cathedral city of ageless beauty and captivating history, Salisbury has been welcoming travellers since 1227.

Tudor building in Salisbury, Wiltshire

Church House, Crane Street

Henry is known to have visited Salisbury twice before, in 1511 and 1514, with Catherine of Aragon. This time it appears he headed with Anne to Church House, Salisbury, the Wiltshire property of John Tuchet, 8th Baron Audley. Contemporary records suggest the welcome was as lavish as Gloucester. They may have lodged in the oldest, southern part of the building, which still faces the River Avon.

Although it has been altered and the interiors extensively remodelled over the years, it retains the sense that it was a great hall befitting a wealthy merchant or gentleman's medieval townhouse. It is a little less grand today, being used as a photocopying room.

Upstairs, although its interiors have been adapted to office life, transforming it into a meeting room, you can see the room that was most likely one of the royal couple's lodging rooms.

Alas, there is little information explaining what happened. There were no notable ceremonies in Salisbury. Historians have speculated they would have received a lavish welcome should they have decided to visit Salisbury and its cathedral.

It's also possible that Anne wanted to see nearby Wilton Abbey. In 1528, she went toe-to-toe with Cardinal Wolsey to elevate Eleanor, the sister of her brother-in-law William Carey, to abbess. She did visit Syon Abbey earlier in the year. Perhaps she was contemplating reformation, or perhaps she simply wanted to pay a visit to Eleanor, her cousin?

Following their visit to Salisbury, Henry and Anne did not continue in a westerly direction, which would have taken them back to Bristol. Instead, they headed eastwards towards the original geists.

Sailsbury attractions

Old Sarum

Castle Road, Salisbury SP1 3SD
www.english-heritage.org.uk

Old Sarum combines the ruins a royal castle and a cathedral within an Iron Age fortification. It was a major centre of both secular and ecclesiastical government for 150 years. Neither the castle nor the cathedral lasted long: in 1226, the cathedral was relocated to Salisbury, while the castle remained an administrative centre into the 14th century. The settlement of Old Sarum survived as a notorious "rotten borough" that continued to elect MPs until 1832.

Salisbury Cathedral

Castle Road, Salisbury SP1 3SD
www.english-heritage.org.uk

This structure is regarded as one of the most important examples of Early English Gothic architecture. Its main body was completed over a 38-year period, from 1220 to 1258. Since 1561, the 404-foot-tall spire, built in 1320, has been the tallest church spire in the United Kingdom.

Visitors can take the "Tower Tour," which allows them to see the interior of the hollow spire, complete with ancient wooden scaffolding. At 80 acres, the cathedral has the largest cloister and the largest cathedral close in the United Kingdom. It houses one of the oldest working clocks in the world, as well as the best surviving of the four original copies of Magna Carta. The cathedral celebrated its 750th anniversary of consecration in 2008.

STOP 23
CLARENDON PALACE
SAT 10 OCT 1535

POSTCODE: SP5 3EW (CAR PARK)

Former royal palace and centrepiece of Clarendon Park, the largest deer park in medieval England, now in ruins.

Ruins of Clarendon Palace, Salisbury, Wiltshire

Clarendon Park and Palace

Henry's letters and papers show that the king and queen planned to visit both Salisbury and Clarendon. Thus, the most likely scenario is they moved the short distance to Clarendon's nearby park and palace, where they stayed until 12 October.

Only ruins remain of this once cherished place of royal pleasure and relaxation in its extensive parks and gardens. Dating from the 12th century, its residential credentials are reinforced by its lake of fortification. Standing in glorious isolation, about 2 miles outside of Salisbury, near the main Southampton–Bristol Road, it was enveloped by the Forest of Clarendon, one of the richest hunting parks in the kingdom, ideal for the nobility sports of hunting and hawking. Moreover, it provided a place of privacy, well away from plague-infested London.

Hunting and hawking are most likely what kept Clarendon as a preferred Plantagenet royal residence until the fifteenth century. There were no such emotional ties for the Tudor monarchs, and thus Clarendon began its inevitable decline. It required work when Henry visited. It is unclear where they would have stayed.

They may have broken the journey at Hurstbourne Priors again during the gap in the records.

Visiting

The ruins of the old Clarendon Palace are open all year.

However, be aware that there are no roads leading up to the site, and it's a fair distance to walk to the ruins from the road.

Ruins of King John's Palace at Clarendon by William Stukeley engraving, 1723

STOP 24

SHERBOURNE ST JOHN
TUE 19 OCT 1535

POSTCODE: RG24 9HL (THE VYNE)

Former Tudor powerhouse turned 17th-century family home, set in gardens, woodlands and wetlands.

The Vyne, Sherbourne St John near Basingstoke, Hampshire

The Vyne

The Vyne, the Sherbourne St John home of William, Lord Sandys, Lord Chamberlain of the Royal Household, was the next destination. The royal couple stayed for around four days.

This was not Anne's first visit to the house; she had been there with Henry when the court spent at least two days there in August 1531. It was also the place where Anne may have conceived for the final time and provided then the much-desired son Henry had hoped for. Henry was clear he wanted an heir—and soon. Anne became increasingly aware that the lack of a healthy son would ultimately lead her to the scaffold.

In its heyday, The Vyne, one of the *'principle'* houses in Hampshire, may have rivalled Hampton Court Palace in size. The building, begun in 1526 and completed two years later, replaced an earlier medieval structure. Then, it was a complex structure with a series of courtyards and a moat. In 1541 it was said to have sixty rooms. The king and queen had their own suites of rooms on the first floor, linked by a gallery and possibly arranged around a courtyard.

There, Anne and Henry spent time with their hosts and courtiers, eating, drinking, and being merry, as described by Francis Bryan in a letter to Thomas Cromwell on the day of their departure.

The Vyne, like so many other grand Tudor houses, was drastically reduced in size, altered, and modernised by subsequent owners, and much of Lord Sandys' house is now buried beneath the lawns north of the current house. As a result, only a few of the sixty or so rooms listed in the 1541 inventory have survived.

The surviving interior features of Lord Sandys' Tudor house are a powerful reminder of a time when The Vyne was one of the greatest houses in Hampshire, and Queen Anne Boleyn was still hopeful of living up to her motto—The Most Happy.

Visiting

For more information on how to get to The Vyne and its seasonal hours, visit the National Trust website.

- www.nationaltrust.org.uk

STOP 25
OLD BASING
TUE 19 OCT 1535

POSTCODE: RG24 7HB (OLD BASING HOUSE)

Ruins of the largest private house in Tudor England which suffered during the English Civil War.

A cannon at the ruins of Old Basing House, Hampshire

Basing House

Basing House was the Hampshire home of Sir William Paulet, Comptroller of the King's Household. Sir William was a wily statesman of incomparable flexibility who would come to serve every single Tudor monarch with assiduous loyalty. It was an expensive visit, costing Paulet an eye-watering £6,000, around £2.6m in today's money. To put that in context, Sir William could have bought 1,263 horses, 4,800 cows, or paid skilled workers to do 200,000 days of work!

Anne and Henry made their way from Sherborne St John to the small town of Old Basing. Sadly, it is another now-ruined stop on the tour, a casualty of an infamous two-year siege during the Civil War, followed by a fire.

The journey was a short one from The Vyne, with the court travelling just five miles in a south-easterly direction.

Approaching from the north, Basing House must have been an impressive sight, more so because this major Tudor building, which eventually rivalled Hampton Court in both scale and opulence, had been undergoing renovations for four years since Sir William was granted a crenelation licence in 1531. Within a short time, Basing was regarded as one of the finest residences in the country. It would come to contain 360 rooms, with some parts of the building rising to five storeys in height. Alas, records for the house are lacking. Historians are left to speculate on what the royal pair may have seen.

For the modern visitor, very little remains visible, except for the outer defensive earthworks of the Old House and some of the foundations of the buildings that once existed within it.

Finally, before you explore this pleasant spot and the traces of a long-lost house, consider the context of the visit and what was going on in Anne and Henry's relationship at the time.

The king is described as *'merry'* on the day the royal couple arrives in Basing, and he may have had reason to be. It is possible that Basing House was another one of the few locations from the latter part of the progress where Anne's longed-for, but fated, son was finally conceived, an intriguing thought!

Visiting

During the winter, the Basing House is closed. For the most up-to-date information on opening hours and prices, please visit the Basing House website.

- www.hampshireculture.org.uk/basing-house

Basingstoke attractions
Milestones Museum

Churchill Way, West Leis Pk, Basingstoke RG22 6PL
www.milestonesmuseum.org.uk

A visit to Milestones in Basingstoke, Hampshire's living history museum, brings the past to life.

The museum houses over 20,000 objects made or used in Hampshire and serves as a record of the county's social, industrial, and transportation history.

Enthusiasts will appreciate the collection of beautifully restored vintage vehicles, while shoppers will be able to see what shops were like before chain stores took over.

Purchase an old penny and a ration coupon at reception to spend in the 1940s sweet shop, or visit Milestones' very own working pub, the Baverstock Arms, which serves teas, coffees, soft drinks, and Gales ales during the lunch hour.

The pub is named after Alton-born scientist James Baverstock, who was among the first to use science to improve the quality of ale.

Photo: Graham Horn

STOP 26
BRAMSHILL
THU 21 OCT 1535

POSTCODE: RG24 7HB (BRAMSHILL HOUSE)

One of the largest and most important Jacobean 'prodigy house' mansions in England. Soon to turn into luxury flats.

The slightly later Jacobean Bramshill House, near Basingstoke, Hampshire

Bramshill House

It appears that Henry and Anne were never supposed to visit Bramshill House. Even as late as 16 October, Sir William Paulet wrote to inform Cromwell that the geists had changed again due to the plague around Alton and Farnham, but Bramshill was never mentioned.

Instead, after a short stay at Basing House, the royal party was scheduled to travel to Elvetham Hall. Sir Francis Bryan's letter to Cromwell two days earlier is the first mention of this turn of events, but there is no record of why the king changed his mind so abruptly.

Elvetham, on the other hand, was another Seymour property, this time owned by Sir Edward, who was beginning to rise in the king's favour. Perhaps, after the stay with the Seymours at Wolfhall, Anne suggested Henry should choose another location.

One of the owners of Bramshill, Lady Daubeney, was Anne's aunt on her mother's side, and records suggest Anne was close to her.

Twenty-four-year-old Katherine had married Lord Henry Daubeney in 1532. Three years later, the marriage was in trouble. Henry had been in poor health for two years and wanted a divorce. Although Daubeney had offered to pay Katherine £100 a year, it may not have materialised since she called on Cromwell to help her financially, saying only her niece was giving her any income. Henry had money worries too. Anne's father, Thomas, now Earl of Wiltshire, loaned him £400. Perhaps Anne wanted to visit to investigate what was happening between the estranged couple?

Bramshill House had a history dating back to before the Norman conquest. On the site now stands a grand Jacobean mansion, dating from 1605. The earlier building, built around a courtyard, had *'broad balustraded terraces, the quaint gardens, and venerable oaks and yews whose branches overshadow the walks'*. Its vaulted cellars matched those of nearby Windsor Castle.

Visiting

Once a former police training centre, the building is now being redeveloped as luxury flats, and is not open to the public.

Wokingham attractions

Photo: Don Cload

Dinton Pastures Country Park

Davis Street, Hurst, Wokingham RG10 0TH
www.dinton-pastures.co.uk

There are 350 acres to explore, including meadows, a fishery, watersports, and conservation lakes. Three public bird hides, an orienteering course, a children's play area, a countryside centre, a small exhibition, and a cafe are all available. There are both dog walking and dog-free areas.

STOP 27
EASTHAMSTEAD
MONDAY 26 OCTOBER 1535

POSTCODE: RG40 3DW (FORMER ROYAL PARK)

Another lost building, located on the south-western edge of Windsor Forest, a former royal hunting lodge since the Middle Ages

St Michael and St Mary Magdalene's Church, Easthampstead, Berkshire

Easthampstead Palace

The next day, they embarked on the penultimate leg of their journey, travelling 10 miles northeast toward Easthampstead in Berkshire. For the long progress, begun sixteen weeks earlier, after a wet summer, winter was now just days away. This stop was another case of visiting a building past its best. Unfortunately, nothing of the building remains. Easthampstead was located on the south-western edge of Windsor Forest and had been reserved for royal hunting since the Middle Ages. A hunting lodge was built by Edward III in the mid-1300s. Richard II, Henry VI, and Richard III all made extensive use of it.

Easthampstead also witnessed another significant event in Tudor history. Henry VII rode out from the royal hunting lodge at Easthampstead to meet the fifteen-year-old Catharine of Aragon upon her arrival from Spain. At this lodge, the gallant Prince Henry first saw his future first wife when they danced together at a banquet, presumably held to celebrate Catherine's safe arrival and the forthcoming wedding with Henry's elder brother, Prince Arthur. Just a few weeks later, on 14 November 1501, the couple were married. Thirty years later, in the same summer that Catherine was expelled from court, Henry and Anne were at Easthampstead, on an earlier progress to Woodstock. Repair records from 1534 and 1535 indicate there were separate lodgings for the king and queen, a chamber for Master Norris', and lodgings for the Marquess of Exeter. There were also references to a Great Hall, chapel, kitchen, and spicery. The staff at Windsor castle maintained the property under the watchful eye of William Sandys, owner of The Vyne. By 1548, the building was apparently in a sorry state and wouldn't make it through another winter. This was mitigated by the excellent hunting and hawking available in 265 acres of prime parkland, teeming with fallow deer. It must have provided fabulous entertainment for the final five days of the progress.

Visiting

Although the manor has gone, you can visit the heart of the old royal park.

South Road, Nine Mile Ride, Wokingham, RG40 3DW is the address.

Sadly, the old palace is now under a golf course.

The nearby Victorian era hotel, Easthampstead Park, Berkshire

THE ARRESTS IN MAY 1536

Anne was beheaded on 19 May 1536, six short months after the progress

Things begin to unravel

Although Anne was almost certainly innocent of any sexual misdeeds, her witty, flirtatious banter with the courtiers, the very quality that had drawn Henry to her in the first place, was one that was easily misrepresented to seal her fate.

On the run-up to May Day, 1536, the court was buzzing with anticipation for the jousting at Greenwich. The king had travelled there on 30 April, while Cromwell travelled into London. But underneath the surface, there was trouble brewing.

Several catalysts have been suggested.

Henry had grown tired of ageing Anne and yet another miscarried boy and wanted to marry Jane, an eligible, fertile woman.

A rival conservative faction wanted to replace the Boleyn faction at court, clip Cromwell's reforming wings and change the succession to Princess Mary.

Another woman at court was accused of adultery, and her idle defensive comment that she was *'not as bad as Anne'* accidentally triggered the sudden investigation.

Henry's intermittent impotence forced Anne to take drastic measures to produce a male heir.

Anne wanted retribution for Henry's wandering eye and mistresses.

Anne hated the double standards at court where a man was *'virile'*, and a mistress was *'contemptible'*, and when her daughter Elizabeth I and her ministers gained access to the archives, the evidence was destroyed.

Centuries later, the matter is still discussed.

Sun 30 Apr 1536
Mark Smeaton's interrogation

The first man to be arrested was Mark Smeaton, the queen's Flemish musician. Historians have raised questions about what happened next, suggesting torture or the offer of a false pardon compelled him to confess.

Victorian historian Hume suggested the torture was Cromwell's handiwork. Strickland suggested a deal was struck with Sir Francis Fitzwilliam.

Cromwell invited Mark Smeaton to dinner at a house in Stepney. Smeaton suspected nothing. Thomas took him by the hand and led him to his chamber, where six men waited.

'Mark, I have wanted to speak to you for some days, and I have had no opportunity till now. Not only I, but many other gentlemen, have noticed that you are ruffling it very bravely of late. We know that four months ago you had nothing, for your father has hardly bread to eat, and now you are buying horses and arms, and have made showy devices and liveries such as no lord of rank can excel. Suspicion has arisen either that you have stolen the money or that someone had given it to you...'

Before his arrest, he was known to lavishly spend on horses and liveries. This was considered suspicious because, as a lowly musician, he only earned £100 per year. Moreover, to his and Anne's enemies, his lavish lifestyle implied that he had received money from the queen in exchange for [sexual] *'services'*.

Kings required assurance that an heir was theirs. Questions about legitimacy were to be avoided at all costs. Queens needed to be faithful. Anne's enemies knew Mark Smeaton could have had ample opportunity to be alone with the queen in her Winchester chamber. Cromwell continued the pursuit of his prey.

'I give you notice now that you will have to tell me the truth before you leave here, either by force or good will.'

Mark became perplexed, then terrified. Cromwell summoned two of his stout young men and demanded a rope and a cudgel. He told them to tie a knotted rope around the musician's head and twist it with the cudgel until he cried out.

'Sir Secretary, no more, I will tell the truth. The queen gave me the money.'

'Ah, Mark,' said Cromwell, *'I know the queen gave you a hundred nobles, but what you have bought has cost over a thousand, and that is a great gift even for a queen to a servant of low degree such as you. If you do not tell me all the truth, I swear by the life of the king I will torture you till you do.'*

'Sir, I tell you truly that she gave it to me.'

Sensing he was getting somewhere, Cromwell ordered a few more twists of the cord, and poor Mark, overcome by the torment, cried out again.

'No more, Sir, I will tell you everything that has happened.'

He said Francis Weston, Henry Norris, and William Brereton had all had relations with Anne

The torture stopped. Cromwell sent Mark to the tower, then penned a letter to the king,

'Your Majesty will recall that Mark has only been in your service for four months and only receives [a £100] salary, yet everyone in the court notices his opulence, and that he has spent a large sum on these jousts, all of which has aroused suspicions in the minds of certain gentlemen, and I have examined Mark, who has made the confession which I enclose to your Majesty in this letter.'

Agnes Strickland put forward the confession explanation, who said that Sir William Fitzwilliam, Henry's Treasurer of the Household and enforcer investigating the case, enticed Smeaton into signing the incriminating deposition.

'Subscribe, Mark, and you will see what will come of it.'

His words hinted that Smeaton would be given a stay of execution but later decided *'it was not fit to let him live to tell tales.'*

Smeaton stated that he was with the Queen on May 13, 1534, at Greenwich. However, she was not in Greenwich on that date but rather in Richmond.

Arrested and taken to the tower at six o'clock in the evening on 1 May, the news caused tremendous controversy with tongues wagging about the queen having physical relations with someone of such low status.

Mon 1 May 1536

The May Day festivities go awry

The May Day jousts were just getting started. Henry read Smeaton's supposed *'confession'*, and the wheels began to turn. Henry insisted the festivities should go on as planned. Then he ordered his boatmen to take him to Westminster.

The queen, unaware that the king had gone, went to the royal balcony that overlooked the tournament and inquired about Henry, only to be told that he was *'busy'*. She also noticed that Smeaton was missing. She was informed he had *'gone to London and had not yet returned.'*

Later that day, Henry issued some orders. *'When the jousts were over, Master Norris and Brereton... should be secretly arrested.'*

Sir Henry Norris's arrest

Prior to his arrest, the king was still treating Henry Norris well, offering his own horse to ride in the May Day festivities. But, alas, it would not turn out to be a day of celebration for the prestigious Groom of the Stool, bailiff of Ewelme and leader of the Boleyn faction. But, as an aristocrat, Norris escaped torture at least.

Henry confronted Norris on the ride back to Westminster, accusing him of an intrigue with Anne and urging him to confess.

Sir William Fitzwilliam then apprehended Norris and brought him to the tower.

There is little evidence that he acted inappropriately with the queen. Norris initially denied his guilt and swore that Anne was innocent. That didn't stop tongues wagging.

There was talk Anne met with Sir Francis Weston in April 1536, who hinted that Norris was in love with her. She had later confronted Norris about it, joking that he was *'waiting for dead men's shoes.'* He objected to the suggestion, thinking it treasonable. Unfortunately for Norris, he had many enemies, and his alleged affair with Anne was meticulously reported to Thomas Cromwell. His downfall was swift.

There is little evidence that he acted inappropriately with the queen. He was interested in marrying another woman at the time, plus his knowledge of the king would have taught him that ruin and death were unavoidable consequences of such desperate adventures.

5pm Tues 2 May 1536

Anne's arrest

The next day, the Captain of the Guard and a hundred halberdiers were dispatched by Henry to Greenwich to take the queen to the tower. Interrupted as she watched a tennis match, she had expected to be taken to meet Henry at Westminster.

By five PM, she was in the tower. Then, she collapsed, demanding to know the location of her father and *'sweet brother'*, as well as the charges against her.

Anne was questioned by four Thomases, Cromwell, Cranmer, Howard, and the Chancellor, Audley. Cranmer offered to show her the confession, and she flew into a rage.

'Go to! It has all been done as I say, because the King has fallen in love, as I know, with Jane Seymour, and does not know how to get rid of me. Well, let him do as he likes, he will get nothing more out of me. Any confession that has been made is false.' She continued, *'My brother is blameless; and if he has been in my chamber to speak with me, surely he might do so without suspicion.'*

Anne complained she would say no more, and the men left. Under considerable strain, Anne began to ramble out loud as she mulled things over. She was accompanied by four unsympathetic ladies in her room. All had been assigned by Cromwell, all with instructions to report on the queen's actions. One of the ladies, Mrs Coffin, did just that with the following information.

When Weston began flirting with Anne Boleyn's cousin, Madge Shelton, he made a fatal mistake for him and Anne. Madge had an affair with the king recently, and her fiancé, Henry Norris, appears to have been hesitant to marry her after that.

Madge was troubled by it, so Anne spoke with Norris before approaching Weston about his unseemly pursuit of Madge. Perhaps Madge's flirtation had gone too far. Anne's had a strict moral code that her servants were expected to follow. Being the king's mistress was one thing, but if Madge became the mistress of a man of Weston's standing, the family's honour would be sullied.

Anne didn't approach Weston and start lecturing him. That wasn't her style. Instead, she chatted with him, using her usual charm. Teasingly, she accused him of being in love with Madge Shelton and not loving his wife. Weston responded that there was someone in her home he loved more than his wife or even Madge: Anne herself.

Anne most likely rolled her eyes and responded with a teasing remark. This was the court's fawning everyday language. Every man was expected to pay homage to the queen and act as if he loved her so much that he was dying of love for her. Poems praising Katharine of Aragon's beauty and begging for a glance were written for her.

Cromwell, on the other hand, was adamant about taking these conversations literally, removing their context and twisting them into admissions of guilt.

Anne later admitted that she was *'more feared'* of Weston's testimony because he was the one who had stated flatly that he loved her rather than implying or being coy about the subject.

She also mentioned asking Smeaton to play some music for her. His discontent was said to have piqued Anne's interest. However, reporting this conversation would be his undoing. Anne admitted that she had once discovered the melancholic musician standing in the round window of her presence-chamber in Westminster.

She asked him why he was so miserable, and he replied defensively, *'It was no matter.'*

'You may not expect me to speak to you as I would to a nobleman,' Anne retorted, *'because you are an inferior person.'*

Smeaton miserably replied, knowing the truth of her words:

'No, no, Madam. A look sufficeth, thus fare you well.'

It wasn't the *'look'* that was the problem, it was Smeaton ending the conversation with *'fare you well'*, which was totally against protocol. Only a monarch could decide when a conversation was *'over'* not a lesser person, and certainly not a commoner.

However, this conversation was quickly contorted and reported to Thomas Cromwell.

With ample time for Smeaton to see Anne at Winchester when she summoned him, this too would have fatal consequences for Smeaton and Anne.

2pm Tue 2 May 1536

George Boleyn's arrest

How times had changed for George Boleyn. In May the previous year, he was a trusted envoy sent to Calais to negotiate a marriage between Princess Elizabeth and the Duke of Angoulême. Now he was facing a treason charge and two counts of incest, one in

November 1535 at Whitehall and the other the following month at Eltham.

His arrest was kept secret and not discovered until the following day. He had arrived at the tower three hours earlier than Anne. The news surprised some courtiers. They assumed he might be in trouble for being Anne's accomplice. When the news of incest was revealed, it was met with shock and disbelief. He may have known nothing about Anne's arrest. Else, he did know and had dashed from Greenwich to Whitehall in a frantic attempt to see Henry. He was definitely at Greenwich as he had given a stellar performance in the jousting.

The four men visited George and told him that he had gone to Anne's room several times at night in just his nightclothes and asked her ladies to leave them alone. He said there was nothing in it, but they felt otherwise.

In the tower, he struggled under the strain ash he awaited his trial. Finally, he asked Kingston, *'When shall I come before the king's council?'* before bursting into tears.

Concerned about him, the Constable of the Tower appealed to Cromwell to assist. He didn't.

Thu 4 May 1536

Sir Francis Weston's arrest

As she muddled through her predicament in the tower, Anne's verbal rants helped the prosecution build a case against Sir Francis Weston. His interrogation by members of the king's council began on May 3, 1536. Vehemently asserting his innocence, he dismissed claims he'd had carnal knowledge of the queen. His protests were in vain. The next day, he was arrested and taken to the tower, with 8 May and 20 May at Westminster and 20 June at Greenwich cited as the places for his transgressions with Anne. They were equally illogical. On the latter two dates, she was with Henry.

Sir William Brereton's arrest

Approaching his fifties, William Brereton was nothing like the other young bucks. Born in 1487, one of seven sons, he entered royal service with three of his brothers and became a Groom of the King's Privy Chamber by 1521. One of his duties was to warm the king's shirt in the mornings, but he would soon be touting for extra tasks that would raise his court profile.

His wife Elizabeth, daughter of Charles Somerset, 1st Earl of Worcester, was one of Anne's gentlewomen. Marrying above his station in 1529, Elizabeth cemented his position as a high-ranking servant.

He received over thirty royal grants in Cheshire and the Welsh Marches as a reward for his loyal service. These eventually brought in a staggering amount of money at that time, more than £10,000 per year. However, he wielded that power ruthlessly, orchestrating the judicial murder of John ap Gryffith Eyton after a string of tit-for-tat murders in the area that had taken out some of Brereton's own henchmen.

Anne was not troubled by William's arrest, thinking there was nothing that would come to light. She was, of course, mistaken.

Brereton was charged with high treason against the king, adultery with the queen, and conspiracy to assassinate the king. Anne solicited him on 16 November 1533, and that misconduct occurred on 27 November at Hampton Court.

Again, the dates were implausible. The queen had just given birth to Princess Elizabeth on 7 September 1533. For the good of her and the baby's health, Anne would have been in seclusion for a few months. Further, at first, Elizabeth was raised at Greenwich Palace, where she was born, not Hampton Court.

Cromwell may have included Brereton in the plot against Anne in order to end the upheavals he was causing in Wales and to reorganise (and centralise) local government in the region

THE ONES THAT 'GOT AWAY'

Three men were arrested after the initial group were detained. They escaped trial. Why might that have been?

Fri 5 May 1536

Sir Francis Bryan's questioning

One of Henry's diplomats, and a courtier who lost an eye in a joust, nicknamed the *'Vicar of Hell'* by Thomas Cromwell, Sir Francis Bryan, was ordered to London for questioning, most likely as a show-off move since he was quickly released.

Related to Anne and Jane Seymour, he was a prominent member of the King's Privy Chamber. Initially removed during Wolsey's purge, he returned in 1528, most likely due to Anne's influence. Later, he appears to have felt no remorse for conspiring with Cromwell to overthrow the Boleyns. Bryan was unquestionably Anne's foe nor friend and profited from the fall of her co-accused.

Sir Francis Bryan was almost certainly never in danger, having joined forces with the Seymours and the anti-Boleyn faction. He had spoken to Henry alone during the visit to Wolf Hall, when Anne had retired early, feeling queasy. Henry complained about Anne upbraiding him in public for having mistresses. Francis was probably hoping to profit from Jane Seymour's rise, just as he had with his other cousin, Anne. He and Jane had always been close. Bryan was the one who got her a position as a maid-of-honour to Catherine of Aragon and then to Anne.

Although he had been a member of the Boleyn group at one point, now his true sympathies were with Catherine of Aragon and Mary. In 1534, he purposefully chose a quarrel with Lord Rochford to distance himself from the Boleyns. Lady Bryan was Princess Elizabeth's governess in 1536, yet, Francis was part of the group encouraging and coaching Jane Seymour.

Bryan was dispatched three hours after Anne's execution to inform Jane Seymour of the news. Later, he succeeded Sir Henry Norris as Groom of the Stool, gaining a share of the spoils.

Mon 8 May 1536

Sir Thomas Wyatt's arrest

Thomas, a poet, diplomat, and friend of the Boleyns, was imprisoned for the same charge but later released, most likely because of his or his family's friendship with Cromwell.

Sir Thomas Wyatt (Cleveland Museum)

He was the son of Henry Wyatt, a Lancastrian supporter in the War of the Roses who rose through the ranks to become a Privy Councillor under Henry VII and a favourite of Henry. In 1516, Thomas entered the King's service and became an ambassador in 1524, following in his father's footsteps. In 1535, he received a knighthood.

Wyatt was claimed to have fallen in love with Anne Boleyn when she first came to the English court in 1522, unhappy in her marriage to Elizabeth Brooke. He was immediately smitten. Anne's eye had already been taken by Henry Percy. As Clerk of the King's Jewels, they would have seen a lot of each other at court.

There is no proof that Anne and Wyatt were dating at the time, and before the Lent of 1526, Anne had a new love—the king. Thomas's love would be unrequited, but later, and even after, some rumours were circulating that there was more to it.

Sources suggest the king sent Cromwell to bring Wyatt in for questioning. Cromwell took Wyatt to one side. Thomas said to him:

'You well know the great love I have always borne you, and I must tell you that it would cut me to the heart if you were guilty in the matter of which I wish to speak.'

Then he told him everything that had happened. Master Wyatt was taken aback.

'Sir Secretary, I have no reason to be suspicious because of the faith I owe to God and my King and Lord, because I have not wronged him even in my thoughts. The King is well aware of what I told him prior to his marriage.'

Cromwell then told him that he would have to go to the tower but that he would stand by his friend.

'I will go willingly,' Wyatt replied, 'because I am stainless and have nothing to fear.'

Nobody knew he was a prisoner because he went out with Richard Williams, Cromwell's protege. When they arrived at the Tower, Richard told the captain Thomas wanted Master Wyatt to receive preferential treatment. He was given chambers above a gatehouse.

His family were worried that his occasional *'vices'* would be his undoing, and a letter was sent to Cromwell suggesting his father was going to make sure he made amends,

He was not called for trial with the other four men on 12 May. Instead, from his window in the Bell Tower, he watched their gruesome executions whilst he awaited to hear of his own fate. By 19 May, his future was still uncertain.

It wouldn't be until nearly a month later, on 11 June, that Cromwell advised his family about Wyatt's release without charge and that his father should help him improve his behaviour.

What saved Wyatt? Despite familiar loyalty, Cromwell would not have had enough clout to secure his release on his own. It seems the king accepted the view that Thomas Wyatt had completely given up on Anne in 1526 when he realised Henry wanted her for himself. Wyatt reminded the king of a *'told you so'* conversation at the time when he warned Henry that Anne would be wayward and unsuitable. It turned out that in 1536 Henry finally agreed.

On 14 June, Henry Wyatt wrote back saying he would do just that. His son had narrowly averted death, and Sir Henry was going to remind him of that.

Sir Richard Page's arrest

Sir Richard Page was related to Henry through his wife Elizabeth Bourchier, the king's cousin. He was a Privy Councillor, and like the others arrested, also on friendly terms with Anne. He performed small courtly services for her that she had repaid with gifts and other tokens. Accusations of an affair with Anne followed.

Page, a former secretary to Cardinal Wolsey, had been knighted in 1529. Opportunistic, he rewarded Wolsey's favour by becoming friends with his foes, the Boleyns. Then, in the 1530s, he became one of Cromwell's favourites.

Like Wyatt, Page's family petitioned for his release. Finally, in June 1536, he too was freed from the tower, but unlike Wyatt, Page was punished by being exiled from court and the King's presence for the rest of his life.

The king, on the other hand, had other ideas and invited Page back. Page stayed away for a while until things calmed down but was coaxed back when Henry appointed him chamberlain to Prince Edward in 1537.

These events imply that not all the investigations were merely a stitch-up, though it is not enough to prove that the others were not rigged. Instead, some historians argue the release was simply a charade to indicate there had been some level of scrutiny in establishing the merits of each case when, in fact, there had no

THE TRIALS BEGIN

Fri 12 May 1536

Smeaton, Norris, Weston and Brereton

Frustratingly, records of the trial are missing, but third-party accounts exist. Before the trial, on May 9, a grand jury convened at Westminster Hall and determined that there was a case to answer for the offences committed at Whitehall. Chief Justice John Baldwin presided over the proceedings, along with six of his colleagues on the bench. On 10 May 10, Baldwin and three assistants travelled to Deptford, where a Kent jury decided there was a case to answer for the events at Greenwich. Cromwell proceeded to arrange the trial for the four receiving the committals.

On 12 May, in Westminster Hall, the jury was packed with people who had reason to be hostile to Anne Boleyn's cause or who had a personal enmity with one of the accused.

- William Askew
  Princess Mary's supporter.
- Robert Dormer
  Opposer of Henry's break with Rome and a Catholic conservative
- Sir Giles Allington
  A son-in-law of Sir Thomas More, executed for his resistance to the break with Rome.
- Walter Hungerford
  A rascal of a man under Cromwell's wing.
- Anthony Hungerford
  One of Jane Seymour's relations, Henry's new love.
- Sir John Hampden
  related to Comptroller of the Royal Household, who was also a judge.
- William Musgrave
  A man who had disappointed Cromwell recently and didn't want to fall short again.
- Thomas Palmer
  Henry's gambling pal.
- William Sidney
  A friend of Charles Brandon and a staunch Mary supporter.
- Richard Tempest
  One of Cromwell's men and an ally of the conservative faction.
- Edward Willoughby as foreman
  Brereton had lent Willoughby money, so it was in his interests to be free of him.

Also present were Anne's father, Thomas Boleyn, her uncle, Thomas Howard, Duke of Norfolk, and the man she had wished to marry 13 years before, Henry Percy, 6th Earl of Northumberland.

One of the judges was Sir William Paulet, the controller of the King's household, the owner of Basing House in Hampshire.

Even without a hostile, hand-picked jury, defendants in a Tudor criminal trial—and especially in a high-profile state trial – were at a significant disadvantage. They were not informed in advance about the evidence to be made public. Denied defence counsel, they were forced to rebut barbed questions from the crown prosecutors, antagonistic men, intent on securing a conviction through means fair or foul.

Smeaton's spending record and a single reported conversation with the queen meant he was quickly found

117

guilty. The date discrepancy in his extracted confession was glossed over.

Norris pleaded not guilty to treason and adultery but was still accused of being solicited by Anne at Westminster on 6 October 1533. Anne was in Greenwich, not Westminster, at the time, recovering from the birth of Elizabeth on 7 September. He was also accused of adultery on 12 October and again in November at Greenwich. In addition to specific charges, there was a catch-all charge of committing adultery 'at various times and locations'. The prosecution's selection of these dates appears highly improbable and hints at carelessness or complacency in their preparation of the evidence.

Before the trial, the Weston family sought an audience with the king or Cromwell. They offered 100,000 marks (the modern equivalent of eight million pounds) for his safe deliverance. Aside from the efforts of the Weston family, Chapuys mentioned a parade of officials attempting to procure a pardon for him. None of this worked. Either the king was determined to press on, or their pleas were not passed on to him. Thus, the death sentence was passed.

He spent his last night writing out his list of debts which are testimony to his lavish lifestyle, his important network at court and his favour with the king and queen. There was even a line listing a debt to a woman for some tennis balls.

When the list was totted up, it was a massive amount, totalling almost £1000. Worth over £300,000 in modern times, it was an amount that could bring financial ruin to a family.

The list was accompanied by a heartfelt farewell letter from the young man, apologising to his parents for the trouble he had caused them:

'Father and Mother,

I shall humbly desire you, for the salvation of my soul, to discharge me of this bill, and to forgive me of all my offences that I have done to you, and in especial to my wife, which I desire for the love of God to forgive me and to pray for me, for I believe prayer will do me good. God's blessing have my children and mine.

By me, a great offender to God.'

Brereton had no witnesses called to testify against him, but was still found guilty.

THE TRIALS CONTINUE

Mon 15 May 1536

The queen and her brother were tried separately within the tower. Anne's case was deliberately scheduled first.

Anne Boleyn

Archbishop Cranmer had visited Anne the morning of the trial, possibly to persuade her to agree to the dissolution of her marriage to the king. However, she likely declined the deal as this would have removed Elizabeth from the line of succession.

The queen was brought to the King's Hall in the Tower of London. In his capacity as Lord Steward, her uncle, the Duke of Norfolk, presided over the court.

Anne's attire and demeanour were daring. She wore an elaborate feathered cap and a black velvet gown with a scarlet damask petticoat. Her body language seemed triumphant. Her head was held high with pride. She bowed down to her judges. She didn't show any outward signs of fear.

As she was publicly accused of incest, adultery, promising to marry Norris after the king's death, conspiring the king's death, and laughing at the king and his dress, Anne listened and remained composed.

She pleaded not guilty and gave clear and dignified answers, denying the charges levelled against her.

After a pretence of proceedings during which Anne defended herself admirably, she was found guilty of all charges.

The Duke of Norfolk, Anne's uncle, then read the final sentence aloud to Anne and everyone present, supposedly with tears streaming down his face:

'Because thou hast committed treason against our sovereign, the king's Grace, and here attained of the same, the law of the realm is that thou hast deserved death, and thy judgement is that thou shalt be burned here within the Tower of London on the Green, or else to have thy head smitten off, as the king's pleasure shall be further known of the same.'

Interestingly, as her sentence was read out, the Earl of Northumberland collapsed and had to be carried out of the hall. Another woman who knew Anne screamed in disbelief. The fact that the queen would be killed was clearly shocking to the public.

Although Anne did not know how she would die, she was no longer left wondering about her fate. She delivered a heartfelt speech to the court after receiving the sentence while remaining composed the entire time. Anne was escorted back to her tower lodgings.

Cranmer may have promised to return, but on 16 May, Sir William Kingston, the Tower constable, wrote to Cromwell, stating that he had not heard from the archbishop and that the queen wanted to hold a confessional.

The execution plans continued apace.

George Boleyn

George, Lord Rochford, stood trial a few hours after Anne. The order of the trials had been deliberately arranged to ensure the difficult case against George could not realistically fail. Since Anne had been found guilty by that point, his fate was already sealed.

Thought to be George Boleyn (Royal Collection)

He could hardly be acquitted when his sister had already been sentenced for incest.

Everyone who witnessed George's trial, including the Imperial Ambassador Eustace Chapuys, considered that he put up a magnificent defence, and many thought he would be acquitted.

Chapuys reported that those watching were betting 10 to 1 that he would be acquitted. His evidence was a marvel to hear. There was no evidence of incest save that he had spent a long time alone with Anne on one occasion.

Chapuys says he was convicted merely on a presumption. Many of the courtiers believed in his innocence, as can be seen from the wagers made in favour of acquittal.

Irrespective of what those at court thought, he was unanimously found guilty, and the sentence of the court was that he be hanged, drawn, and quartered (the sentence was later commuted to beheading).

He asked for his debts to be paid out of his confiscated assets so that no one would suffer from his death, and he continued to be distressed about his finances whilst awaiting execution. So acute was the distress that Kingston wrote to Cromwell again begging him to help ease George's conscience.

EXAMINING THE TRIALS

It was as if the evidence was crafted to damn the accused no matter what had happened.

Historians pondering the question of innocence point out that Tudor palaces had strict protocols in place that meant a queen would need assistance to meet up with a lover. Three wives later, Katherine Howard relied on Lady Rochford's to help smuggle Thomas Culpeper into her privy. Even if Anne could meet someone, meeting multiple men frequently was doomed to failure. The repeated unexplained absences would hardly be a secret. A telling clause that accompanied the dates in the evidence was *'diversis aliis diebus et vicibus antea et postea'*, a catch-all phrase meaning '[and other] other days and times, before and after'. The wording suggested that Anne was never forced into the liaisons, else she might have the defence of being violated. Calling the offences treasonous was also a stretch. Intercourse with a consenting queen was not treason under English law. A wife killing her husband was guilty at common law of petty treason, but it was only a misdemeanour to deceive him. Adultery was dealt with in the church courts. Thus, the May 1536 trials expanded the treason law in novel and oppressively retroactive ways.

The only legal substance the indictments had was in the concluding stories, which claimed that the king's life had been jeopardised because Anne had destroyed the men's loyalty with gifts, which led them to conspire to kill Henry. According to the 1352 statute, causing harm to or plotting against the king was unquestionably treason. It's debatable how justified the 1536 accusations were. Henry's shock was brief. Chapuys remarked on how quickly he bounced back from the *'betrayal'*.

The effect of the rumour mill

Courtly stories inevitably spread. What matters most is their dependability. The letters of William Kingston, Constable of the Tower, detailing Anne's conversations there, are the most authoritative. Some of them were most likely courtly love clichés, like Francis Weston's empty flattery that he loved Anne more than his wife or would-be mistress. Other revelations were more serious in nature.

The queen's spat with Norris in late April enraged courtly sensibilities. Her behaviour made her the talk of the court. Her challenge to Norris, 'that if ought came to the King but good, you would look to have me,' was transformed in the indictment into a promise to marry one of the plotters should the King die. This lent credence to the crown's most damaging accusation: intending the king's death. Kingston's letters also clearly attribute Smeaton's mooning around the palace to Anne, almost inviting interrogation.

Ladies-in-waiting statements

Soon, rumours about rumours circulated. The upcoming revelations by the ladies of Anne's household were hotly anticipated. Supposed corroboration from the ladies was limited to three instances. They were reported on by Justice John Spelman, who was present at Anne's trial.

Lady Bridget Wingfield (Deceased)

Bridget Wingfield had been close to Anne, but the court never heard her deposition, only a report of what she allegedly said on her deathbed. At that point, she had been dead for at least two years.

For those who were alive, being an ostrich was not advisable. The conventional wisdom on what courtiers should do with dangerous knowledge was clear.

'Say it as soon as possible because the longer you keep it, the worse it will be for you.'

Why hadn't Lady Wingfield's dark revelations been made public sooner, and who had kept them hidden until the right time?

Another example is Anne's gentlewoman Margery Horseman. On 3 May, Anne's vice-chamberlain Sir Edward Baynton (he of Bromham House on the tour), advised that Margery should be questioned immediately. This is puzzling because, after Anne's death, Margery served Henry's third wife. Would Henry really be willing to have Margery near Jane if she had been suspected of helping Anne be unfaithful?

Jane Boleyn, Lady Rochford

Many people believe that Jane Boleyn, widow of George, was to blame for initiating Anne's fall. However, it has never been proved that she set the wheels in motion regarding Anne's downfall. Jane has been called a *'pathological meddler'*. She encouraged the relationship between wife number five, Catherine Howard, and Thomas Culpepper. If Jane had anything to do with Anne's downfall, she must have realised that she was lucky to escape in 1536, and if she didn't then, she doesn't seem to have learnt anything from the whole affair.

If it was not Jane Boleyn, then who was it?

Elizabeth Browne, The Countess of Worcester

Elizabeth is also considered to be a main source of gossip regarding tales of Anne's misconduct.

The Countess was reprimanded by her brother for her behaviour, to which she replied that she was 'no worse than the queen'. In another instance, Elizabeth herself criticised a lady-in-waiting by likening her behaviour to that of the queen.

In another, Elizabeth suggests that her brother talked to Mark Smeaton and a lady-in-waiting about Anne's behaviour.

In the April or May of 1536, there is strong evidence others were saying much the same.

Who said what to whom regarding the betrayal of Anne Boleyn remains shrouded in mystery. Finally, however, someone put the wheels in motion, and the intimate details of what was going on and what was said in Anne's bedchamber came from someone close to Anne.

Who was it then who instigated such dangerous conversations? Where does Cromwell fit in?

Did someone plant the seed in Henry's head that he needed to be rid of Anne? If so, who? The Seymours. The conservative old guard? Cromwell? Was it the king's own conclusion? Did Henry or someone else see to it that a loose cannon at court got the ball rolling, someone who could get the loose talk to flow in court about Anne's *'behaviour'* so it could be used against her?

Some material was certainly obtained from Anne's staff. The prosecution was aware of Anne's letter informing Rochford that she was pregnant, his visit to her room, sister kissing brother, gifts to Norris, courtiers competing for her favour, and Anne's dislike of being shone down by other women in her own court. A lot of this was normal behaviour, typical of family life at the time, or a display of *'courtly love'*, widely accepted at the time. Yet, gifts may appear suspicious when taken out of context. Similarly, what is expected behaviour within a convention can be made to appear suspicious later on.

That said, certainly, Anne's circle was pushing the boundaries of decency. Lady Rochford's revelation of discussions about the king's sexual inadequacy and possibly what she thought of Henry's dress and poetry was a major embarrassment. Elizabeth could not be Henry's daughter, joked George Boleyn. This confirms the impression given by Anne's revelations from the tower that she had allowed a *'pastime in the queen's chamber'* to become out of hand by the end of April. Perhaps Anne was hoping to make Henry jealous, or maybe the feverish atmosphere was an instinctive reaction to the emergence of a rival court centred on Jane Seymour.

This all oiled the wheels to create a case sufficient to quieten the general public and satisfy wavering consciences with the help of *'innuendo and implication'*. The telling of stories lost nothing in the telling, and no doubt, the widespread dislike of Anne and the assumption that she began as Henry's ambitious mistress aided in guiding minds to the right *'conclusion'*.

A jumble of court and popular stories with little substance but with the potential to be manufactured into a case against them rapidly materialised in apparent corroboration of the Crown's case, which seemed to be an official version of the rumour.

Observers agreed that although the accused sounded extremely convincing in their defence, their denials were dismissed.

Cromwell's role and motives

One unanswered question in all of this is Thomas Cromwell's place and role. Historical understanding is based on the minister's own admission to Chapuys, less than a fortnight after Anne's death, that he had orchestrated her demise due to a dangerous disagreement with Henry over a possible imperial alliance.

Of course, ambassadors were easy targets for disinformation, and everything Cromwell told Chapuys could be dismissed as a *'negotiating technique.'*

When looking at a motive for the king's right-hand man, after George Boleyn's execution, Cromwell took over as Lord Privy Seal and gained a valuable stewardship. His servant Sir Ralph Sadler received William Brereton's freehold estate near Greenwich. When Sadler died in 1587, he was reputedly *'the richest commoner in England'*.

It could be argued, however, that a political or diplomatic development demanded Anne's removal. As well as clashing over the redistribution of wealth during the Dissolution, with Anne favouring helping charities, they were at odds over a French alliance. Cromwell insisted on replenishing the king's depleted coffers (while pocketing a cut for himself). He also preferred an imperial alliance with Charles V. The emperor was Catherine of Aragon's nephew and wanted the alliance to put Mary next in line to the throne, not Elizabeth.

Charles V

These conflicting objectives made Anne a threat to Cromwell.

Henry made it clear that he expected Charles to recognise that his relations with the pope were his own affair, something of which Anne was a symbol, as was Mary's future.

Remove Anne, and for Cromwell, both problems vanish.

However, Cromwell would be vulnerable without Anne to the conservative faction that despised him equally. They, too, wanted a return to pre-reformation life. Cromwell's dissolution angered them, as it was being used to increase the power of commoners over the nobility. Joining this faction temporarily was a way to destroy Anne was to save himself.

Self-defence would also explain the inclusion of Rochford and Norris; attempting to remove the Queen while her allies were still powerfully placed around the king would have been folly.

A faction vying for preferential treatment is a feature of personal rule, whether by Henry or Joseph Stalin.

The supposed Catholic faction

A series of courtiers hostile to Anne may have already been instilling suspicions in the king's mind and then manoeuvred into position to drive the case against her. The events were a legal travesty by modern standards; however, the rules of the time were not bent in order to ensure a conviction.

Was there a hidden faction?

Despite the powerful indications of innocence, there was also undeniable evidence of a deliberate intent to destroy Anne and the others. The case against them was built from a mishmash of court and popular rumour with little substance, yet it formed a potent case against them. How were incontrovertible facts, for example, the date and location conflicts for the alleged offences, ignored?

Sufficient evidence was clearly lacking to prove Anne, and at least some of her male friends were guilty.

There is another hypothesis that Anne's downfall resulted from an underground political coup and a classic example of a Tudor faction at work. This explanation stands up better to scrutiny. Anne's fall happened despite strong indications of innocence, and there is undeniable evidence of a deliberate intent to destroy her and key members of the Boleyn faction.

The clues that there may have been a faction at the helm come from two letters written by Ambassador Chapuys. One example was written on

1 April 1536, well before any investigation into Anne, that Henry's interest in Jane Seymour was growing.

Princess Mary's succession case was openly debated in the Privy Chamber within days of the Boleyn arrests. When it became clear that Henry would not legitimise Mary, their activities also became the subject of an investigation. Given there was evidence of damaging activities before and after Anne's fall, it would be absurd not to recognise a group plotting and promoting her demise to usher in the Seymour marriage and Mary's restoration.

The faction's motives probably included dislike of the Boleyns, respect for the Aragon marriage, and hostility to recent attacks on the church, but their objectives could also be seen primarily in personal interest terms, which is exactly the thing a faction fights for—its own self-interest.

The commission of the arrest had the hallmarks of a chancery initiative which Henry knew nothing about. On 24 April, Henry was at Greenwich, and to personally approve paperwork for the case would have meant an unplanned journey to Westminster where it was issued. A messenger could easily have brought the text downriver if Henry had been personally involved, and a Greenwich mark would have been applied instead. On 25 April, a contemporary account says Henry was still writing of Anne as *'our most dear and most entirely beloved wife'*.

This minor point in legal procedure suggests that someone other than the king was in charge, triggering Henry's break with Anne after 25 April but before the end of the month, when the court's schedule and tone was abruptly changed.

Low-born Smeaton was clearly a pawn, easily sacrificed to hasten Anne's fall. However, the situation was different with George and Sir Henry Norris. Anne, her brother, and Sir Henry formed a formidable trio in key positions in the king's entourage. Further, although less influential, William Brereton was also on the privy chamber staff, had powerful influence in the Welsh Marches, had strong connections with Anne, and was involved in the patronage game with Norris. All of them needed to fall for the faction's coup to succeed.

The existence of this conspiratorial group was no proof of its power beyond sabotaging Anne's position. Moreover, later events in 1536 strongly suggest the group lacked potency.

The shock of May 1536 rippled on at court throughout the summer. Within a matter of weeks, Henry rounded on the successful faction, and there was a further bout of arrests and interrogations, although, this time, no executions.

In June, Mary was forced to accept that her parent's marriage was invalid and publicly relinquish her claim to the throne. At the October Pilgrimage of Grace in northern England, a rebel uprising numbering 20,000 to 40,000 men and a host of northern nobles hoping to reinstate Mary, amongst other things, resulted in two hundred high profile executions for treason, including their leader, lawyer Robert Aske.

Henry's psychology

However, there is one element that will never be fully explained - Henry's mind.

The faction may have conspired to throw him off balance in 1536, as it had on previous occasions, but it was the King who listened.

Without a doubt, the main reason was his crippling suspicion, which was his greatest failing; but what else could have allowed a pack of lies to destroy years of consistent and public support for Anne so dramatically and instantly?

His faith in a male heir by her had been temporarily shaken by the January miscarriage.

Had that apprehension lingered in the subconscious?

How about Jane Seymour?

Was the King trapped by a heavy flirtation; was he asserting his right to do whatever he pleased, or was he provoked by Anne's objections?

All these possibilities have been considered, but we simply do not know.

And isn't there something almost pathological in a man who, after publicly rejecting a woman he'd been in love with for ten years, then becomes deeply involved in the details of killing her?

All discussion of Anne Boleyn's downfall leads to the ultimate unsolvable paradox of Tudor history: Henry VIII's psychology.

Later, in 1542, parliament effectively admitted that the crown had acted outside of its constitutional authority by making adultery with a queen a treasonable offence.

THE EXECUTIONS BEGIN

Wednesday 17 May 1536

Execution of George Boleyn, Norris, Weston, Brereton and Smeaton

After being found guilty, all four men were sentenced to death by hanging, drawing, and quartering. Later, clemency prevailed, and the sentence was reduced to beheading.

As the most high-ranking of the four men, George was first to face the axeman. His lengthy scaffold speech demonstrated his confidence in his linguistic abilities. For it to have been recorded in such detail, the vast crowd that witnessed the executions had to have been virtually silent, with little booing or jeering as with normal state executions.

He followed the convention of the day by admitting he was a sinner deserving of death. He begged forgiveness from anyone he might have offended, as well as forgiveness from God.

He came close to denying his guilt when he said, *'Beware, trust not in the vanity of the world or the flatteries of the court, or the favour and treacheries of fortune.'* He claimed that if he had not done so, he would still be alive.

By blaming fate for his fall, he came as close to denying his guilt as he dared, suggesting he was dying because luck had been against him, not because he was guilty. As well as exposing those left behind to harsh repercussions, denying a guilty verdict was seen as grossly dishonourable.

He then spoke of his religious beliefs before calmly submitting his neck to the axe. Some reports said three blows were needed to finish the job.

Unlike the other accused, who used carefully chosen words to demonstrate their innocence, Norris did not want to risk reimposing the harsher method of execution and thus said little on the scaffold.

According to Sir Robert Naunton, Queen Elizabeth I always remembered him, believing he died *'in a noble cause and in the justification of her mother's innocence.'*

Little has survived about Francis Weston apart from saying:

'I had thought to have lived in abomination yet this twenty or thirty years and then to have made amends. I thought little it would come to this.'

Similarly, Brereton said:

'I have deserved to die if it were a thousand deaths. But the cause whereof I die, judge not. But if ye judge, judge the best.'

Some say his reference to '1,000 deaths' referred to his heavy-handed rule in the Welsh Marches.

The final man was Mark Smeaton. His sentence had been commuted to beheading rather than the brutal handing, drawing, and quartering usually reserved for commoners. The reason is thought to have been his cooperation with Anne's enemies. Still, it must have been horrifying to witness three violent deaths before him, knowing he too only had minutes to live. As he was led to his execution, Smeaton staggered back from the bloody scaffold, no doubt because it would be awash with blood and butchered bodies. His voice faltered as he spoke to the crowd. He did not take the opportunity to retract his confession before he was dispatched. His final words were:

'Masters, I pray you all pray for me, for I have deserved the death'

When Anne heard of this, it angered her.

'Has he not then cleared me of the public infamy he has brought me to? Alas, I fear his soul suffers for it, and that he is now punished for his false accusations!'

The men's corpses *'were allowed to lie on the scaffold for hours, half dressed'* before they were stripped and prepared for burial.

Norris, Weston, Brereton, and Smeaton, as commoners, were buried together in the churchyard of the Chapel of St Peter ad Vincula. As an aristocrat, George Boleyn's remains were buried separately by the high altar.

Years after Smeaton's death, Queen Mary convinced herself that her sister, Elizabeth, was illegitimate, the result of Smeaton and Anne's alleged affair. She stated on several occasions that Elizabeth had the *'face and countenance'* of Smeaton. However, Elizabeth's close resemblance to Henry was so obvious that Mary had little success convincing others, and the accusation died with her.

Friday 19 May 1536

Execution of Anne Boleyn

From the Bell Tower or the Byward Tower, both of which were high enough to provide a view of Tower Hill, according to one of Anne's ladies in attendance, the queen watched the bloodbath below. Carpenters were soon dispatched to nearby Tower Green to erect a scaffold for Anne high enough to allow all those present to see.

After, Ambassador Chapuys learned Anne would now be executed on 18 May, a day later than planned. The news filtered through to Anne, who returned to the queen's quarters.

Kingston then informed her sentence was commuted from burning to beheading. Rather than have a former queen beheaded with a common axe, Henry had an expert swordsman coming from Saint-Omer, France, carry out the execution.

Kingston reported she seemed very happy and ready to be done with life. Curious to hear what the men who had just been executed had said, Anne asked if they had expressed any doubts about her innocence. He advised her they had not.

Noon had come and gone. The execution was postponed until the next morning to provide enough witnesses for the spectacle. Again, Kingston informed Anne, who expressed her dissatisfaction. This time, Anne begged Kingston to stop the execution, but he was powerless to do so.

Archbishop Cranmer convened a court in Lambeth Palace between nine and eleven o'clock in the morning. Both the King and Anne were summoned to the court, but neither of them showed up. Along with other lawyers, Cranmer declared Henry and Anne's marriage null and void, either because of Anne's pre-supposed contract with the Earl of Northumberland or Henry's earlier affair with her sister Mary. From this point on, Elizabeth was referred to as Lady Elizabeth rather than Princess Elizabeth. Although some sources claim that he prepared Anne for death by hearing her last private confession of sins, in which she stated her innocence before God, he made no serious attempt to save Anne's life.

The fallen queen devoted her time to prayer and consolation for her ladies and had a sleepless night.

At dawn, Anne heard mass. She held her last confession with Kingston, swearing in his presence, on the eternal salvation of her soul, upon the Holy Sacraments, that she had never betrayed the king. She received the sacrament, then ate breakfast. Kingston knocked on her door at 8 o'clock that morning to inform her that the hour was approaching. Anne was mentally prepared to accept her fate once more and told him of her readiness. Kingston gave her £20 to give as alms. The condemned was expected to pay the executioner, but the king had already made arrangements.

Kingston wrote of the encounter:

'I told her it shouldn't hurt...then she said she'd heard the executioner was very good, and I have a little neck, and put her hands around her neck, laughing heartily. I've seen many men and women executed, and I've seen them in great pain, but this lady, to my knowledge, takes great pleasure in death.'

Finally, the hour cometh. Anne had given a lot of thought to her clothing and appearance. She wore a red damask skirt with a black or grey damask robe. She was also dressed in a mantle made of royal ermine. The robe's low neckline meant she didn't have to take it off for the executioner to do his job.

Anne emerged from her lodgings, aided by Kingston, accompanied by four ladies. They were joined by two hundred Yeoman of the Guard in a procession to Tower Green. The executioner and his assistant awaited them away from the scaffold, the sword tucked away in the straw that covered the wooden boards.

Now there were plenty of witnesses—over 1,000. Among those present were Thomas Cromwell and members of the king's council. Henry's illegitimate son, Henry Fitzroy, and joint friend Charles Brandon, 1st Duke of Suffolk, stood by. The Dukes of Norfolk and Suffolk, other earls, nobles, and lords, the Lord Mayor of London, aldermen, sheriffs, and representatives from various craft guilds, looked on.

When Anne appeared, the crowd erupted in applause, and witnesses described her as stunning. Anne distributed the alms as she walked through the crowd. Kingston assisted her up the scaffold steps, and her ladies trailed behind. Anne gazed around the crowd before approaching Kingston and asking for permission to speak, which was granted. Eyewitnesses said she spoke to the crowd from the scaffold with grace and a voice that was a little weak at first but grew stronger as she went on.

'...if I ever offended the king's grace in my life, I'm sure I've made amends with my death. I have come here to accuse no one, nor to speak of the charges against me, because I am well aware that nothing I say in my defence will be of any use to you. I pray and beseech you all, good friends, to pray for the king's life, my sovereign lord and yours, who is one of the best princes on the face of the earth, who has always treated me so well that nothing could be better, wherefore I submit to death with good will, humbly asking pardon of all the world. If anyone is going to interfere with my cause, I expect them to make the best decision possible. As a result, I bid farewell to the world and to you, and I humbly request that you all pray for me. Please, Lord, have pity on me! I offer my soul to God.'

Like most people who faced execution at the tower, Anne needed to avoid any suggestion of criticism of the monarch to protect her child and her wider circle of family and friends from repercussions after their death.

Anne turned around and inquired about the executioner. She was advised he would be there shortly. Anne removed her gabled hood, and her ladies removed her mantle. One of the women handed her a linen cap. Then, tucking her long hair into it, she exposed her neck. Anne thanked her ladies for their help and asked them to pray for her.

The executioner approached and asked for her forgiveness, which she readily granted. He told her to get down on her knees and pray. With the execution by sword, there was no need for a block. She requested time to pray. She kept adjusting her cap, worried it would get in the way. With compassion, the executioner reassured her she didn't need to remove it, and he would wait until she was ready.

On her signal, one of her ladies stepped forward to blindfold her eyes. Except for the Dukes of Suffolk and Richmond, the entire crowd knelt as she awaited the blow. The events unfolded quickly. The headsman walked over to the scaffold steps and motioned for his assistant to bring the sword to him. Anne shifted her gaze to the stairwell, her hand still clutching her cap.

The executioner raised the sword out of the straw and walked up to Anne barefoot so she would not hear his approach as she repeated the same prayer.

'Jesu receive my soul; O Lord God have pity on my soul.'

With the sword clasped in both hands, he circled it around his head for momentum and brought it down, severing her head from her neck in an instant.

The head landed in the scaffolding's straw. One of the ladies covered it with a white handkerchief. The death was signalled by the firing of cannons along Tower Wharf.

The severed head was taken by one lady as the other three wrapped the body in a white cloth and placed it in a chest previously used to store archery bows.

The chest was taken inside the Chapel of St Peter ad Vincula on the tower grounds. A cleric blessed the body, then she was buried beneath an unmarked chancel flagstone that afternoon.

Archbishop Cranmer had a busy day ahead of him, issuing a dispensation for Henry to marry Jane Seymour without first publishing banns.

During Queen Victoria's reign, her skeleton was discovered during chapel renovations in 1876, and Anne's grave is now marked on the marble floor.

THE REMAINDER OF THE REIGN

Henry's third marriage, Jane Seymour

The day after Anne's execution, Henry, 45, became engaged to Seymour. Stephen Gardiner, Bishop of Winchester, married them ten days later in the queen's closet at the Palace of Whitehall, Whitehall, London. Jane gave birth to a son, Prince Edward, the future Edward VI, on October 12, 1537. The birth was difficult, and Queen Jane died of an infection 12 days later and was buried in St George's Chapel, Windsor.

The euphoria that had accompanied the boy's birth soon gave way to sorrow, yet Henry had little time to recover from the shock. At the insistence of Cromwell and the Privy Council, measures were immediately put in place to find Henry another wife, with a focus on a powerful alliance with one of the powerful European households.

Cromwell's fall

After the trials, Cromwell's position was stronger than it had ever been. On 2 July 1536, he succeeded Anne's father, Thomas Boleyn, as Lord Privy Seal. He was elevated to the peerage as Baron Cromwell of Wimbledon on July 8, 1536.

He continued with his Dissolution work. After the break with Rome, the first attempt to clarify religious doctrine was also made in July 1536.

Bishop Edward Foxe presented proposals which received strong support from Cromwell and Cranmer and were later endorsed by the King as the Ten Articles. They were printed and distributed in August 1536.

Cromwell circulated injunctions for their enforcement that went beyond the articles themselves, provoking opposition in Lincolnshire and then throughout the six northern counties in September and October. This anger of the northern nobility and the gentry triggered the Pilgrimage of Grace. The rebels had many grievances, but the most important for Cromwell's future was the suppression of the monasteries, which they blamed on the King's *'evil counsellors'*, primarily him and Cranmer. During his interrogation, one of the rebel leaders, Baron Thomas Darcy warned Cromwell that his ingratiation with the king and his tendency to overstep his remit would bring about his undoing.

Undeterred by the warning, Cromwell felt the suppression of the risings prompted additional Reformation measures. He called a synod of bishops and academics together in February 1537. Cranmer helped coordinate the meeting. By July, they had completed a draft document called *'The Institution of a Christian Man'*, also known as *'the Bishops' Book'*. It was in circulation by October, though the King had not yet given his full approval. On 5 August 1537, the King reaffirmed his support for Cromwell by inducting him into the Order of the Garter

Cromwell declared open war on the proponents of the old religion and their *'idolatry'*, launching an extensive campaign against them. In January 1538, statues, rood screens, and images were destroyed. In September, St Thomas Becket's shrine in Canterbury was desecrated. More injunctions followed, one ordering that *'one book of the whole bible in English'* be installed in every church.

Furthermore, after the *'voluntary'* surrender of the remaining smaller monasteries the previous year, the larger monasteries were now *'invited'* to surrender throughout 1538, a process legitimised in the 1539 session of Parliament and completed the following year.

At the same time, the King was becoming increasingly dissatisfied with the extent of religious changes. The conservative faction at court was growing in strength.

Cromwell took the initiative in dealing with his adversaries. In November 1538, he imprisoned the Marquess of Exeter, Sir Edward Neville, and Sir Nicholas Carew on treason charges. Evidence of their guilt had been obtained from Sir Geoffrey Pole during interrogation in the tower. The three men accused of the *'Exeter Conspiracy'* were executed. Sir Geoffrey was pardoned despite being *'broken in spirit.'*

Production of the new English bible was prohibited by the Inquisitor-General of France on December 17, 1538. However, Cromwell persuaded King Louis XVI of France to release the unfinished books, allowing printing to resume England. The first edition of The Great Bible was published in April 1539. The first authoritative version in English, it was one of Cromwell's major achievements.

The king continued to oppose further Reformation measures. A parliamentary committee was formed to investigate doctrine and in 1539. The Duke of Norfolk presented six questions to the house for consideration, which were duly passed as the Act of Six Articles, which reaffirmed a traditional (i.e., a more Roman Catholic) interpretation of the mass, sacraments, and the priesthood.

Henry's fourth marriage, Anne of Cleves

The final straw for Henry's patience with Thomas was the arrangement of his marriage to Anne of Cleves, who Henry later dubbed *'The Flanders Mare'*.

It had been two years since Queen Jane died in 1537. Then, in early October 1539, the king finally agreed to Cromwell's suggestion that he marry Anne of Cleves, the sister of Duke Wilhelm of Cleves, partly because of a flattering portrait of her painted by Hans Holbein. After that, Cromwell often spoke to Henry of her beauty.

Anne of Cleves arrived in Dover on December 27th. On New Year's Day 1540, the King met her at Rochester and was physically repulsed by her: '*I like her not!*'

Despite Henry's obvious displeasure, the wedding ceremony took place in Greenwich on January 6, but the marriage was not consummated. Henry stated that it was impossible for him to have conjugal relations with a woman he found '*so unattractive*'.

Cromwell had proven himself to be a shrewd political survivor in 1536, successfully transitioning to the Seymour faction. However, the King's more gradual conversion to Protestantism combined with Cromwell at the helm of the ill-fated marriage to Anne of Cleves proved costly.

Miraculously, Cromwell survived the international embarrassment caused by the failure to conjugate the marriage at first. Henry granted Cromwell the earldom of Essex and the senior court office of Lord Great Chamberlain on April 18, 1540. Unfortunately, the bestowal of these favours was short-lived. Cromwell's time as the King's chief minister was drawing to a close.

Cromwell's conservative opponents, most notably the powerful Duke of Norfolk, had hoped for an opportunity to exploit the king's rage at being duped into marrying Anne of Cleves.

Cromwell was initially one of only two courtiers to whom the king confided that he had been unable to consummate the marriage, and Sir William Fitzwilliam, Lord High Admiral Southampton, who had brought Anne across the Channel.

Southampton made certain that Cromwell was held responsible for revealing the king's most intimate of humiliations. Previously loyal to Cromwell, the self-serving disloyalty indicated that the chief minister's position was known to be deteriorating.

Cromwell's management of foreign policy also got him into hot water with the king. The Franco-Imperial Catholic alliance had failed to materialise. Henry dispatched the Duke of Norfolk to the French court of King Francis I to offer his support in his unresolved dispute with Emperor Charles V. The mission had been well received. This shifted the balance of power in England's favour on the continent. It also demonstrated that Cromwell's previous policy of seeking an alliance with the Duchy of Cleves had resulted in his king's public humiliation.

Early in 1540, Cromwell's religiously conservative, aristocratic opponents, led by the Duke of Norfolk and supported by Stephen Gardiner, Bishop of Winchester, dubbed '*Wily Winchester*' for his mischievous counsels to the king, decided that the country's decline towards religious radicalism should be reversed.

They saw an opportunity to depose Thomas in the form of Catherine Howard, Norfolk's niece. Situations were engineered to draw Catherine to the king's eye and thereby claw back power from Cromwell.

Cromwell's survival was complicated. He could have easily arranged an annulment of Henry's unconsummated marriage to the agreeable Anne, but this would have put him in even more jeopardy. Henry being a single man once more, would have cleared the way for Catherine to marry the king. Cromwell's shepherding two important revenue bills through parliament meant he clung onto power for a little longer.

His opponents began whispering in the paranoid king's ear that Thomas needed to go.

Cromwell was arrested and charged with various offences during a council meeting on June 10, 1540. His opponents took every opportunity to humiliate him, even ripping off his Order of the Garter, remarking, '*a traitor must not wear it.*'

His first reaction was defiance: '*This then is my reward for faithful service!*' he cried out, defying his fellow councillor's label.

Now, it was Cromwell's turn for a stint in the tower.

A Bill of Attainder was introduced into the House of Lords a week later, containing a long list of indictments, including corrupt practises leniency in matters of justice, acting for personal gain, protecting Protestants accused of heresy and, and plotting to marry King Henry's daughter Mary.

Two days later, it was augmented with a new charge of sacramentarianism, for which the Six Articles only allowed the death penalty. It became law on June 29, 1540.

All of Cromwell's honours were stripped away, and it was publicly declared that he could only be known as '*Thomas Cromwell, cloth carder.*'

Henry postponed the execution until his marriage to Anne of Cleves could be annulled; Anne, with remarkable common sense, happily agreed to an amicable annulment and was treated generously by Henry as a result.

In his final, personal address to the king, Cromwell wrote in support of the annulment, hoping for clemency. However, the note ended with a begging tone: '*Most gracious Prince, I cry for mercy, mercy, mercy.*'

Cromwell was sentenced to death without a trial, stripped of all his property and powerful titles. On the day Henry married Catherine Howard, July 28, 1540, Thomas was publicly beheaded on Tower Hill.

He gave the customary damage limitation speech to protect his family, in the form of a prayer, declaring that he would die '*in the traditional [Catholic] faith*' and denied he had aided heretics.

The circumstances of his execution are disputed: some accounts claim that the executioner had great difficulty severing the head, having to hack away at it. Others argue that this is apocryphal propaganda and that only one blow was required.

Following that, his head was placed on a spike on London Bridge.

Less than a year later, Henry came to regret Cromwell's execution and later, with the French ambassador noting the king accused his ministers of bringing Thomas's downfall through '*pretexts*' and '*false accusations*'.

Henry's fifth marriage, Catherine Howard

Catherine Howard (1521) was Anne Boleyn's cousin and the powerful Duke of Norfolk's niece. She was young, pretty, and full of life.

By the time she met Henry, he was middle-aged, obese, plagued by injuries and had developed a terrible habit of turning on his wives when they did not meet his lofty expectations. As a result, his attention was soon drawn to Catherine Howard, a cousin of Anne Boleyn, who was a lady-in-waiting to Henry's former wife, Anne of Cleves.

Youthful Catherine was pushed by her family into the king's attention, who decided she was exactly the sort of wife he had been looking for—despite the thirty-year age gap.

Henry and Catherine were married on 28 July 1540, just three weeks after his marriage to Anne of Cleves was annulled.

Catherine faced many challenges as a young bride, including the fact that she was at least two years younger than Henry's elder daughter Mary. Further, Henry expected high moral standards in his wives, if not for himself.

It was rumoured that Catherine had an ambiguous sexual past. This was probably deliberately concealed from Henry before the wedding, as he would have deemed his betrothed unworthy of a king.

Catherine's mother died when she was young. Around 10 or 12 years old, she was sent to live with her step-grandmother, Agnes Howard, the Dowager Duchess of Norfolk. The duchess didn't pay much attention to Catherine's upbringing. The girl was reportedly subject to the advances of her music teacher, Henry Mannock, a music teacher twice her age, and a minor noble, Francis Dereham, who had called her *'his wife'*.

Tragically, her chances of keeping it secret were dashed when (in likelihood) she made the mistake of having an affair with Thomas Culpepper, a Gentleman of the King's Privy Chamber. Few concrete details have been found, but it was reportedly her maid, Jane Boleyn, brother George's widow, who helped Catherine meet with Thomas.

Rumours of Catherine's affair reached Thomas Cranmer. Further investigations into Catherine's past quickly followed, and the King was informed of Catherine's pre-marital behaviour and alleged infidelities at Hampton Court Palace on 2 November 1541.

Catherine was charged with leading an *'abominable, base, carnal, voluptuous, and vicious life, like a common harlot, with diverse persons'*. Henry was reluctant at first to believe anything and passed the allegations off as idle rumour and gossip. It seems that he may have been willing to forgive Catherine for her past before their marriage, but the case of an affair proved too much.

Later that month, she was stripped of her title as queen. Charged with adultery, the young queen was placed under house arrest at Hampton Court, and from there to the tower, on 10 February 1542. On the way may have seen the rotting heads of Culpepper and Dereham, which were displayed on London Bridge.

Hampton Court's Haunted Gallery owes its name to the story of the ghost of Catherine. It is said she managed to escape from her rooms and run along the gallery to the Chapel Royal where the king was at Mass. But, before she could reach him, she was seized by the guards and dragged screaming back to her rooms. It is said that her ghost still shrieks along the gallery.

She was beheaded at the tower on 13th February 1542.

Henry's sixth marriage, Katherine Parr

Katherine Parr was the daughter of Kendal's Sir Thomas Parr and his wife, Maud Green, and a descendant of King Edward III's son, John of Gaunt. The couple married Henry on 12 July 1543 at Hampton Court Palace.

Katherine demonstrated her ability to restore Henry's court as a family home for his children. She was determined to present the royal household as a close-knit unit to demonstrate strength through unity to Henry's opposition.

Perhaps Katherine's most significant accomplishment was encouraging Henry's passing of an act that confirmed both Mary's and Elizabeth's line in succession for the throne, even though both had been rendered illegitimate by divorce or remarriage. Such was Henry's faith in Katherine that he appointed her to rule as regent while he was attending to the war in France, and she was to serve as regent until nine-year-old Edward came of age in the unlikely event of his death.

As her second marriage came to an end, Katherine used her late mother's friendship with Catherine of Aragon to renew her own friendship with Princess Mary. By 16 February 1543, Catherine had established herself as a member of Mary's household, and it was there that she drew the king's attention. Despite her romantic friendship with Sir Thomas Seymour, the late Queen Jane's brother, she felt obligated to accept Henry's proposal over Seymour's. To remove Seymour from the king's court, he was assigned to a position in Brussels.

Katherine survived Henry, who died the following year, going on to marry Seymour and residing at Berkeley Castle.

Despite Henry's considerable effort to bolster the Tudor dynasty's succession, his son Edward was only nine years old when he died.

Edward VI

Having sons remained a priority for Henry until the end. England's peace and prosperity depended on the fruit of his wives' wombs. But, alas, children died quickly in Tudor times and having one son was not enough.

Henry's own younger brother, Arthur, had died when he was fifteen. Henry's illegitimate son, Henry Fitzroy, died aged 17. Edward fell ill during January 1553 with a fever and cough that gradually worsened. By February, the diagnosis was terminal. He and his council drew up a *'Devise for the Succession'* to prevent the country's return to Catholicism. He attempted to defy his father's wishes by leaving the throne to his Protestant cousin Lady Jane Grey, great-granddaughter of Henry VII, excluding Catholic Mary and her younger Protestant half-sister, Elizabeth, from the succession.

Even though Mary could have sought refuge with family members in Europe, she chose to stay in England and fight for what was rightfully hers. She evaded her opponents' armies by rallying support from nobles across the country and marching on London. Mary and Elizabeth rode side by side into England's capital, one as a queen and the other as a queen-in-waiting. Lady Jane Grey was arrested and executed at the tower for treason on 12 February 1554.

During her five-year reign, Mary faced numerous challenges as the first English queen to wear the crown in her own right, rather than as the wife of a king. She placed religion first and foremost, enacting reforms and restrictions aimed at restoring the Catholic Church's dominance in England. Most notably, she ordered the burning at the stake of 280 Protestants as heretics, cementing her reputation as *'Bloody Mary.'* After a long trial and imprisonment, Thomas Cranmer was forced to proclaim to the public his error in supporting Protestantism, an act designed to discourage followers of the new religion. Despite his announcement, he was sentenced and burned to death in Oxford. In a dramatic show of defiance, he thrust his right hand into the flames, the hand that had signed his recantation.

There were more positive pieces of policy in the short five-year reign. Mary established precedents and laid the groundwork for initiatives such as financial reform, exploration, and naval expansion, all of which were built on by her much-lauded sister. Although she married three times, Mary failed to fulfil what is arguably that most important duty of any monarch: producing an heir. She had a phantom pregnancy with her husband, Philip II of Spain.

She died at the age of 42 in 1558 of an illness, possibly cancer of the uterus.

Elizabeth

At the age of 25, Elizabeth ascended to the throne. She kept it until she died 44 years later, in 1603.

During her reign, she re-established Protestantism in England, defeated the Spanish Armada in 1588, survived several assassination attempts, kept peace within her previously divided country, and created an environment conducive to the arts. She, unlike her father, never married.

Henry could never have predicted that all three of his children would reign, nor that his youngest daughter would become one of England's greatest, longest ruling monarchs, nor that within sixty years, his beloved Tudor dynasty would fizzle out.

TUDOR FOOD

Overview

Many people associate Tudor food and eating habits with actor Charles Laughton's portrayal of Henry tossing a greasy, gnawed chicken leg over his shoulder. But, instead, people in Tudor England had a strong sense of table manners and ate a varied diet, even if they didn't think it was necessary to get their *'five a day.'*

The Tudor diet relied heavily on red meat, particularly beef. According to Thomas Cogan's The Haven of Health from 1589, *'beef of all flesh is most usual among English men,'* while physician Andrew Boorde believed that beef *'doth make an Englishman strong'* once salted. In addition, farm animals and wildlife grown entirely on pasture and other greenery would have had a rich flavour. Mutton was the second most popular meat, followed by capons—immature castrated male chickens—and pigeons. Pig meat, formerly inexpensive and widely available, fell out of favour in the sixteenth century, whereas rabbit consumption skyrocketed. The affluent Willoughby family of Wollaton Hall employed their own *'coninger'*, Thomas Hill, who earned his nickname from *'conies'* which meant full-grown rabbits.

Those at the top of the social ladder, particularly the monarch, had access to a variety of other foods, including venison, pheasant, partridge, quail, swan, goose, and stork. The turkey,

137

our Christmas bird, was an exotic novelty. It was first mentioned in reports in the 1570s.

Sixteenth-century meals were high in butter, cheese, and eggs, which were consumed with copious amounts of bread. One of the best breads was 'white manchet,' prepared with fine white wheat flour and occasionally laced with chalk.

Meat was not consumed on fast days, which were every Friday and Saturday, as well as throughout Lent and Advent, except on Sundays. Instead, the Tudors ate salted fish like cod, ling, and pollock, as well as fresh fish like haddock, turbot, and plaice. In addition, there were vast amounts of oysters for sale in London. Fruits and vegetables were regarded as bad for man's digestion, inviting an upset stomach or *'fostering foul humours'*. Such attitudes naturally supported a relatively low intake of fruits and vegetables for those who could afford to avoid them, but the kitchen garden was still a part of every diet to some level.

Depending on the seasons, Tudors could grow and eat apples, pears, damsons, peaches, oranges, lemons, and berries, as well as cabbages, beans, peas, leeks, turnips, onions, and parsnips. Carrots were still in their infancy, and potatoes were yet to arrive in Henry's time. Pottage, a broth, or stew of whatever meat was available with leeks, onions, herbs, and the local cereal grain was a filling meal for the poor.

Water was also regarded to be bad for digestion, so most people drank ale, made of water and malted grain, or else beer, a foreign, hop-infused drink. Wine was a high-end import. The wealthy drank French wines from Gascony or Bordeaux, sherry, or sweet Malmsey wine from Greece.

Other edible treats were enjoyed by those at the pinnacle of society. Popular sweetmeats of Henry's court included marchpane, an early variant of marzipan made of crushed almonds, rosewater, and sugar. *'Subtleties'* were complex modelled embellishments, most fashioned out of a form of sugar paste, occasionally with the addition of wax. A ruse was to build life-like nuts or cinnamon sticks out of sugar paste coated with cinnamon or serve wine in a sugar goblet. Once the wine was gone, the goblet could be eaten.

To impress visiting French ambassadors in 1527, Wolsey served up *'so many dishes, subtleties, and curious devices, which were above a hundred in number, and of such goodly proportion and cost, that I suppose the Frenchmen never saw the like.'*

His novelties included a chessboard made of *'spiced paste'* and a model of the then-St Paul's Cathedral. If that wasn't enough sweetness, the king and queen also loved hippocras, a spiced wine with sugar dissolved in it. It's no surprise that many wealthy Tudors had blackened teeth!

MAKE A TUDOR RECIPE

A bowl of frumenty

Frumenty

Frumenty was a staple food in the 16th century. Before potatoes arrived, it was served as the carbohydrate part of the meal. Roast and boiled meat, fish and game were all served with it through the Middle Ages, Tudor, and Stuart periods. There are many versions, including a savoury winter dish often served at Christmas. It was symbolic, a sign that spring would come. Later, it became a festival dish served on Twelfth Night, 5 January. This sweet dish is made with ale, cream, eggs, currants, and spices.

Equipment

- ☐ A saucepan
- ☐ A mug
- ☐ A spatula

Ingredients

- ☐ 140 g (5 oz) bulgar wheat
- ☐ 1 pint of ale
- ☐ 1 large or 2 small eggs, beaten
- ☐ 1 to 2 handfuls of currants
- ☐ ½ teaspoon (or generous pinch) of cinnamon, nutmeg, and ginger
- ☐ 3-4 tablespoons of single cream
- ☐ a mug of water to top-up during cooking (if required)

Preparation

1. Either soak the wheat in the ale overnight until it swells up or boil for 15 mins stand for 15 mins.
2. Add the spices to the wheat, then boil for a few mins until the wheat is soft.
3. If all the ale is absorbed as it cooks, add a little water
4. Remove from the heat.
5. Add currants and leave to cool a little.
6. Stir in beaten egg(s) and cream.
7. Cook on a low heat. Do not allow it to boil.

PACKING LIST

Some handy prompts for things you might want to take with you on your trip. Over time, think about what you needed and didn't have with you and what you did have but didn't use to refine your list each time. Try to keep things in the same place, so they're easy to find and store, else chaos reigns.

Lastminute packing

Check batteries a few days before you go, so there's time to charge them.

- ☐ Rechargeable batteries
- ☐ Rechargeable power packs
- ☐ Headtorch/torch batteries
- ☐ Camera battery
- ☐ Mattress air pump
- ☐ Car battery booster pack
- ☐ Jump leads
- ☐ Electronics cables/adapters
- ☐ Camper interior lights
- ☐ Power inverter
- ☐ Electric hook up lead

Essentials

Keep these handy...

- ☐ Money
- ☐ Wallet
- ☐ Credit card
- ☐ Phone/GPS

- ☐ Phone charger
- ☐ Camera
- ☐ Personal medication(s)
- ☐ Snacks
- ☐ Beverages
- ☐ Paper towels/napkins
- ☐ Plastic bags/sheets

Paper backups

In case there's no signal or your phone goes flat...

- ☐ Important phone numbers
- ☐ Booking confirmations
- ☐ Tickets
- ☐ Printed directions
- ☐ Maps and guides

Travel comfort

- ☐ Hat
- ☐ Gloves
- ☐ Sunglasses
- ☐ Regular glasses
- ☐ Sweatshirt

Lastminute packing
Get these close to your camp

- [ ] Cooler ice
- [ ] Cold/hot drinks
- [ ] Takeaway meal
- [ ] Fresh water
- [ ] Milk

Personal hygiene

- [ ] Toothbrush and paste
- [ ] Floss
- [ ] Mouthwash
- [ ] Deodorant
- [ ] Hand sanitiser
- [ ] Shampoo (regular and dry)
- [ ] Body wipes
- [ ] Bodywash
- [ ] Flip flops (for showers)

Healthcare

- [ ] Contacts, case, and solution
- [ ] Chapstick
- [ ] Sunscreen
- [ ] Shaving cream
- [ ] Razor
- [ ] Comb/Brush
- [ ] Anti-allergy tablets
- [ ] Upset stomach medicines
- [ ] Pain relief
- [ ] Antiseptic cream
- [ ] Plasters and bandages

Bathroom necessities

- [ ] Towel
- [ ] Brush/Comb/Sponge
- [ ] Toilet paper (biodegradable)
- [ ] Cassette toilet & chemicals
- [ ] Bucket/Bivvy loo
- [ ] Rubbish bag

Clothes/Outerwear

- [ ] Underwear
- [ ] Socks
- [ ] Long/short sleeve shirts
- [ ] Long/short trousers
- [ ] Waterproof clothes
- [ ] Sweatshirt/Hoodie
- [ ] Pyjamas
- [ ] Hat (sunhat or woolly)
- [ ] Walking boots
- [ ] Spare/smart shoes
- [ ] Swimwear

Essential camp kit

- [ ] Window blinds
- [ ] Tailgate lock
- [ ] Anti-condensation granules
- [ ] Doormat for muddy shoes
- [ ] Awning/tent, poles, and pegs
- [ ] Mallet
- [ ] Tarpaulin/Groundsheet
- [ ] Paracord
- [ ] Fold-out roof awning
- [ ] Hammock
- [ ] Lighter/matches
- [ ] Swiss Army knife
- [ ] Pop-up toilet/storage tent
- [ ] Water storage (collapsible)
- [ ] Rechargeable cooling fan
- [ ] Tent sealer/repair kit
- [ ] Microfibre towels
- [ ] Rooftop cargo bag
- [ ] Solar panel and leads
- [ ] Solar/USB shower
- [ ] Hot water bottle
- [ ] Barbeque

Sleep gear

- [ ] Pillow or other padding
- [ ] Sleeping bag/duvet
- [ ] Sleeping mat
- [ ] Extra blanket
- [ ] Pet bed
- [ ] Cot

Drinks

- [ ] Coffee/Tea/Sugar
- [ ] Hot chocolate mix
- [ ] Powdered milk
- [ ] Cold drinks

Dinnerware

- [ ] Folding table and chairs
- [ ] Bowls
- [ ] Plates
- [ ] Mugs
- [ ] Cutlery
- [ ] Drinking glasses

Cookware

- [ ] Stove and spare fuel
- [ ] Fuel hoses and adapters
- [ ] Kettle
- [ ] Pans
- [ ] Cutting block and knife
- [ ] Serving spoon
- [ ] Tongs
- [ ] Can opener
- [ ] Aluminium foil
- [ ] Ziplock bags
- [ ] Paper towels
- [ ] Washing up liquid
- [ ] Collapsible washing up bowl
- [ ] Insulated bag for picnics/takeaways

Repairs

- [ ] Duct tape
- [ ] Cable ties

Cleaning

- [ ] Dustpan & brush
- [ ] Old towel
- [ ] Something to mop up spills
- [ ] Bag for wet/muddy gear

Hobbies

- [ ] Use your own list for these prompts
- [ ] Hiking
- [ ] Running
- [ ] Swimming
- [ ] Kayaking
- [ ] Cycling
- [ ] Photography
- [ ] Videography
- [ ] Bluetooth speaker
- [ ] Fishing
- [ ] Late night walks
- [ ] Musical instrument
- [ ] Puzzles and games
- [ ] Reading
- [ ] Downloaded TV/Films
- [ ] Writing
- [ ] Drawing
- [ ] Painting
- [ ] Crafts
- [ ] Plant ID book
- [ ] Wildlife ID book
- [ ] Binoculars (bird watching)
- [ ] Pens/pencils
- [ ] Notebook

Important things to bring
Jot down some notes of what you want to take with you

PHONE APPS AND WEBSITES

Apps

Travelling by car apps

Google Maps
Add *'near me'* to your search to find local matches for your searches, for example *'chip shops near me'*. You can download an area beforehand.

Waze
Good for live-traffic up updates.

PetrolPrices
Find the nearest, cheapest fuel.

What3words
Great for finding rural places. More accurate than using the postcode.

Circuit
Used by delivery drivers to find the most efficient route between waypoints. Great for planning a stage to take in the places you want to see.

Public transport apps

Google Maps
Great for planning buses or trains if you fancy a break from driving.

UK Bus Checker
Excellent tool for telling you when a bus is due at your stop.

Train Track
Another great tool for telling you when a train is due and which platform.

Walking apps

OS Maps
Good for exploring green spaces.

Komoot and GoJauntly
Suggestions for recreational biking and walking routes.

E-Walk
Excellent for finding shortcuts and green spaces in urban locations.

Where is Public Toilet
Handy for finding places in shopping centres, cafes, and shops.

Cycling

CycleStreets and BikeMap

Route planning services for cyclists with settings for mountain and road bikes.

History

National Trust, English Heritage, Historic Houses Association

Lists the details of their properties such as prices, opening times, parking, and facilities.

Entertainment apps

Remember to download what you want to watch before you go away to save your data.

- Alexa (read Kindle books aloud)
- Kindle
- Netflix
- Amazon Prime
- SkyGo
- TV channel players
- Podcasts
- Ticket booking
- Viator
- Ticketmaster
- Skiddle
- Eventbrite
- Bandsintown

Camping apps

Camping membership apps

For the clubs you are a member of.

Searchforsites
Find places to stop when out and about and for places to park up overnight.

Archies
A large database of UK campsites.

Packpoint
Handy packing list app so you can make sure nothing important gets left behind. Add your own custom lists to the suggested essentials.

Key websites

Tourism

These sites are handy for checking for further details before you visit.

- www.nationaltrust.org.uk
- www.english-heritage.org.uk
- www.cotswolds.com
- www.visit-hampshire.co.uk
- www.visitgloucestershire.co.uk/
- www.visitengland.com

Camping

Online site directories

- www.coolcamping.com
- www.pitchup.com
- www.campsites.co.uk
- www.ukcampsite.co.uk/sites
- campingandcaravanningclub.co.uk
- www.caravanclub.co.uk

HANDY TIPS FOR MICROCAMPING

Take extra fuel for cooking

The most common type of stove uses butane or propane gas canisters. Make sure you have ample supplies. You might get through more than you think, especially on cold or windy days, and not every campsite has a shop.

Take an insulated picnic bag

Great for bringing takeaways home hot, else for bringing frozen food and water bottles from home, so it keeps cold for a bit longer out of the fridge. Remember too that the fuller your bag is, the better it will maintain its temperature.

Have a cooking essentials box

It's easy to forget things like spatulas, scissors and bottle or can openers, so pack a kitchen utensils box to take with you. Look out for multi-tool utensils like large *'sporks'* that can flip, drain, serve or stir food.

Take something to light your stove or BBQ

If you stay at a campsite that allows barbecues make sure you take something to light it with. Also, a handy backup to your cooker ignition system.

Plan meals in advance

This helps you bring the right long-life foods with you to make a meal in an emergency, and it helps makes sure you have the right utensils and pans for your meals.

Use spray oil for cooking

A small amount of spray oil in a travel bottle is much more convenient for cooking than taking a huge bottle from home.

Take a folding water carrier

A collapsible water carrier that easily dispenses water is a camping must-have. Pans and people need a rinse every now and again. In addition, a collapsible carrier wastes less space as you use the water.

Collect condiment sachets

Amazon and eBay, and bargain home stores sell lots of foodstuffs in sachets. Sometimes, you might be given some extras at a fast food joint—salt, pepper, sauces, jams etc. The handy miniature sizes make them ideal for cooking on the road.

Take a hot water bottle

A hot water bottle is a great way to keep warm in your car or van. Even the best quality sleeping bag will benefit from the extra heat generated, helping you sleep well instead of lying awake shivering all night.

Take a lantern

Whilst torches have their place, if you want to relax, a lantern will provide a more practical and soothing light source. If you forget to bring one, point your torch at a filled water bottle, and it will diffuse the light.

Fairy lights as night lights

Battery-powered fairy lights produce a lovely gentle glow and look pretty. Pick a set with a remote control, so it's easy to switch them on and off when you're in bed. If you're careful, you can twizzle spiral upholstery pins into your roof fabric or use magnets with hooks to pin them up. Alternatively, see if you can push the metal handle of small bulldog clips in between the upholstery or headliner fabric to hold up the wire.

Make sure you know how to pitch your awning before you get to the campsite

On a relaxed sunny afternoon, pitching a new awning isn't such a headache, but imagine getting stuck in traffic, arriving late and then the heavens opening. It also allows you to pay attention to how your awning is packed, so you stand a fighting chance of getting it back in the bag the same way. Take some photos as you unpack it the first time. If you forget, don't worry; manufacturers' videos on YouTube usually explain more.

Unzip windows and doors to put your awning away

You're less likely to trap air in the fabric, and it will fold up smaller.

Bring a pair of slip-on shoes

These are handy to put on if you need to pop outside quickly.

Take a waterproof door mat to stand on

In wet weather, your camper can quickly get muddy. Having a doormat acts like a bit of a barrier helping to keep the inside of your car dry and clean. Also, have a bin bag handy to store muddy footwear.

Keep a camping essentials box always packed

Put together your own camping essentials box and include things like duct tape, a multi-tool, first aid kit, torch, matches and so on. That way, you'll know you've always got those random things that you always seem to need.

Use jumbo shopping bags for packing

These make packing a doddle. They are large enough to fit sleeping bags and pillows inside, and transporting in bags like this means if you are setting up or taking down in the rain, your camping gear won't get wet. Use different colours for different things, it helps keep things organised.

Take something to charge your essential devices

A USB battery pack is ideal for charging up your phone if you're using it for navigating or entertainment. Look for one over 10,000 mAh to do multiple charges. You can use a 240v inverter with a 3-pin plug socket to charge up low-power devices like laptops as you drive.

Take cleaning wipes for spills

Kitchen roll and microfibre tea towels are great for dealing with mishaps.

Pack extra layers

Regardless of the time of year, dressing in layers is a good idea when it comes to spending time outdoors. Make sure you've got plenty of warm layers, waterproofs and so on.

Pay attention to how you pack your car

When you pack the car, make sure the things you will need first are easily accessible. That means you won't have to unpack everything before you can get to them—especially handy if you end up having to set up in the rain.

Bring the right sleeping bag

Like your duvet at home, sleeping bags have a tog rating that tells you how well insulated it is and how warm it is likely to keep you. A cheap one-season sleeping bag is very light and unlikely to keep you toasty unless it's summer. Instead, look for a three- or four-season bag to ensure you'll be comfortable in the colder months. A bag with an integral hood is great for winter too. Else bring a woolly hat just in case you need it.

Don't go to bed cold

If you're prone to cold feet, if you get into your sleeping bag cold, you are likely to stay chilly. Before you go to bed, have a warm drink, or go for a brisk walk to the toilet block to warm up your core temperature a little before settling down for the night.

Use a sleeping bag liner

Consider buying a bag liner. These are said to add an extra *'season'* of warmth. They come in silk or flannel material and are an easy way to adjust the temperature of your bag when you're on the road.

Invest in some heat packs

Heat packs are useful. Popping a couple in your pockets can make a real difference. There are chemical ones that are single or multi-use, or you can get rechargeable USB electric ones.

Quick tips

- Use strong neodymium magnets to connect awnings to cars and hang things up.

- A mosquito net can cover your tailgate to stop midges coming in. Handy for those Scotland trips...

- A hanging shoe rack or back-of-seat organiser is handy for keeping frequently used items close to hand and out of the way.

- Bring some loose change for parking meters and small purchases like coffees or snacks.

- 7-day pillboxes with flip-top lids are good for storing a selection of herbs. Just relabel the lids with the name of the herb or spice rather than the day.

- Sachet hot chocolate or coffee drinks with milk and sugar are handy for hot drinks as they don't need chilled milk.

- If you have a gym membership with a large chain, you've got access to a shower.

- A 12-volt car kettle is good for hot drinks, as well as cuppa soups and pot noodles. It takes around 15 minutes to boil the water and needs the car engine running, so you can only use it when you're travelling, but with a bit of planning, it's a great alternative to getting the gas cooker out when you arrive somewhere.

- A microfibre towel is good for dealing with window condensation. Cut down on the amount that forms by putting condensation gel bags under the seats and insulating your windows with blackout blinds.

- Car window wind deflectors and tailgate locks are good for leaving the windows and tailgate open a little a night.

- Scope out coffee shops in the area if you need good WiFi and mains power. Get loyalty apps for food and drink shops to help find them and check what facilities they have.

- Take a portable jump-start in case you get stranded somewhere. Some of them also double up as backup power for your phone or tablet.

- Check your owner's manual to make sure you know how to turn the alarm and any interior lights off. Practice before you go away.

- Build a wooden sleeping platform so you can store things underneath your bed/seating area. Look up '*boot jumps*' on the internet for ideas. You can also make your own simple set-up with heavy-duty plastic storage boxes with an inflatable mattress on the top. Check Facebook groups and YouTube for lots more tips from other campers.

- Use a 12-volt bento box (like a heated lunch box) to heat canned meals as you drive. For example, hot dogs are nice and easy to reheat quickly. So are crumpets with butter. Remember you'll need to keep the engine running to use your bento box, so switch it on in good time as you travel so you can eat when you arrive.

- Get the most out of google maps by searching for '*XYZ near me*' and '*XYZ along the route*', for example, '*petrol stations along the route*'.

- Consider getting a cheap tablet for doing research on the road. It's less fiddly than fighting with a tiny phone screen—and it's good for watching films too. In addition, you can '*tether*' your tablet to your mobile phone, so you can share the internet connection.

- If you need to do a lot of typing when you're away, invest in a Bluetooth keyboard and mouse to go with your tablet to save taking a bulky or expensive laptop with you.

ROAD TRIP GAMES

Spotting things

Allocate some points for spotting things as you drive along:

- A private number plate
- A field of cows or sheep
- A yellow vehicle
- A specific road sign, for example, *'no right turn'*

Word games

The list game

- Pick a category and take it in turns to add an item to the list, for example, *'places ending in -cester, -caster or -ceister'*. They are usually on the site of former Roman settlements.

The rhyme game

- Pick a word, then take it in turns to say things that rhyme with it.

PLACES TO EAT

Abingdon

The Plum Pudding
££ - £££   Bar British Pub
www.theplumpuddingmilton.co.uk
44 High St, Milton, Abingdon OX14 4EJ

The Greyhound
££ - £££   Bar British Pub
www.greyhound-besselsleigh.co.uk
Besselseigh, Abingdon OX13 5PX

The Barley Mow
££ - £££   Pub Vegetarian Friendly Vegan Options
www.chefandbrewer.com
Clifton Hampden Rd, Abingdon OX14 3EH

Dil Raj
££ - £££   Indian Asian Balti
www.dilrajabingdon.co.uk/app/
6 Ock St, Abingdon OX14 5AW

Mahee Tandoori
££ - £££   Indian Asian Balti
maheetandoori.co.uk
15 Bridge St, Abingdon OX14 3HN

Dorindo's Mexican Restaurant
££ - £££   Mexican Vegetarian Friendly Vegan Options
dorindos.co.uk
15 High St, Abingdon OX14 5BB

Hugomangos
££ - £££   Asian Thai Vegetarian Friendly
hugomangos.co.uk
12 Ock St, Abingdon OX14 5BZ

Throwing Buns
£   Quick Bites Cafe British
throwingbuns.com
8 Market Place, Abingdon OX14 3HG

Bromham

The Greyhound
££ - £££   Bar British Pub
www.thegreyhoundbromham.co.uk
High St, Bromham SN15 2HA

The Haveli Indian Restaurant
££ - £££   Indian Vegetarian Friendly Vegan Options
haveliindian.co.uk
71 St. Ediths Marsh, Bromham SN15 2DF

The Prince of Wales
££ - £££   Bar British Pub
www.princeofwalesbromham.com
8 Northampton Rd, Bromham MK43 8PE

Chippenham

Jollys Irish Cafe
£ Quick Bites Irish Cafe
www.facebook.com/jollyirishcafe
18 Market Place, Chippenham SN15 3HW

Grounded Chippenham
££ - £££ Quick Bites Bar Cafe
www.cafegrounded.co.uk
1 Bath Rd, Chippenham SN15 2BB

Fortune Inn Bar & Chinese Restaurant
££ - £££ Chinese Asian Pub
115 Sheldon Rd, Chippenham SN14 0DA

The Gladstone Arms
££ - £££ Bar British Pub
www.thegladstonearms.co.uk
34 Gladstone Rd, Chippenham SN15 3BW

The Garden
££ - £££ Bar British Vegetarian Friendly
thegardenuk.co.uk
15-17 The Bridge, Chippenham SN15 1HA

Athena Meze Bar & Restaurant
££ - £££ Mediterranean European Greek
www.athenamezerestaurant.co.uk
66 New Rd, Chippenham SN15 1ES

Rivo Lounge
££ - £££ Quick Bites Bar Contemporary
www.thelounges.co.uk
2-4 The Bridge, Chippenham SN15 1EX

The George Inn
££ - £££ Bar Pub Vegetarian Friendly
www.facebookTheGeorgeInnSandyLane/
Sandy Lane, Chippenham SN15 2PY

Gloucester

The Red Lion
££ - £££ Bar British Pub
www.redlionwainlode.co.uk
Wainlode Ln, Norton, Gloucester GL2 9LW

Greek On The Docks
££ - £££ Mediterranean Greek Vegetarian Friendly
www.greekonthedocks.co.uk
Gloucester and Sharpness Canal, Merchants Quay, Gloucester, GL1 2EW

Indian Memories
££ - £££ Indian Asian Balti
www.indianmemories.co.uk
79 Bristol Rd, Quedgeley, Gloucester GL2 4NE

The Fountain Inn
££ - £££ Bar British Pub
www.thefountaininngloucester.com
53 Westgate St, Gloucester GL1 2NW

Aroma Indian Restaurant
££ - £££ Indian Asian Vegetarian Friendly
www.aroma-gloucester.co.uk
69 Southgate St, Gloucester GL1 1TX

Peppers Coffee
£ Quick Bites Vegetarian Friendly Vegan Options
www.facebook.com/peppersglos
2 Bull Lane, Gloucester GL1 2HG

Lily's
££ - £££ Cafe British Vegetarian Friendly
www.lilysrestaurant.co.uk
5A College Ct, Gloucester GL1 2NJ

King John's Hunting Lodge
££ - £££ British Vegetarian Friendly Vegan Options
www.kingjohns.co.uk
21 Church St, Lacock SN15 2LB

Lacock

George Inn
££ - £££ Bar British Contemporary
www.georgeinnlacock.co.uk
4 West St, Lacock SN15 2LH

The Carpenters Arms
££ - £££ Quick Bites Bar British
carpentersarmschippenham.co.uk
22 Church St, Lacock SN15 2LB

The Red Lion Pub
££ - £££ Bar British Pub
www.redlionlacock.co.uk
1 High St, Lacock SN15 2LQ

Sign of the Angel
££ - £££ British Vegetarian Friendly Vegan Options
www.signoftheangel.co.uk
6 Church St, Lacock SN15 2LB

The Rising Sun
££ - £££ Bar European Pub
risingsunlacock.co.uk
32 Bowden Hill, Lacock SN15 2PP

The Bell
££ - £££ Bar British Pub
www.thebellatlacock.co.uk
The Wharf Bowden Hill, Lacock SN15 2PJ

Marlborough

Pino's Ristorante
££ - £££ Italian Pizza Vegetarian Friendly
www.pinosristorante.co.uk
13 New Rd, Marlborough SN8 1AH

Mercer's of Marlborough
££ - £££ Cafe British Healthy
www.facebook.com/MercersOfMarlborough
Unit B Hilliers Yard, Marlborough SN8 1BE

Rick Stein
££££ British Vegetarian Friendly Vegan Options
rickstein.com/restaurants/rick-stein-marlborough/
Lloran House 42A High St, Marlborough SN8 1HQ

The Bell at West Overton
££ - £££ Bar British Pub
www.thebellwestoverton.co.uk
99 Bath Rd, Marlborough SN8 1QD

The Food Gallery
££ - £££ Quick Bites Cafe British
www.thefoodgallery.co.uk
48 High St, Marlborough SN8 1HQ

The Who'd A Thought It
££ - £££ Bar British Pub
thewhodathoughtit.co.uk
High St Lockeridge, Marlborough SN8 4EL

Dan's at The Crown
££ - £££ European British Vegetarian Friendly
www.dansrestaurant.co.uk
6-7 The Parade, Marlborough SN8 1NE

The Swan
££ - £££ Bar British Pub
www.theswanwilton.com
Grafton Rd, Wilton, Marlborough SN8 3SS

Porchester

St. Mary's Church Tea Room
£ Cafe British Vegetarian Friendly
www.stmary-portchester.org.uk/tea-room
Church Rd, Portchester PO16 9QW

Reading

Coconut Bar & Kitchen
££ - £££ Japanese Asian Thai
www.coconutbarkitchen.co.uk
St Marys Butts, Reading RG1 2LG

Spice Master
££ - £££ Indian Asian Balti
www.spicemasterreading.com
22 Hildens Dv Tilehurst, Reading RG31 5HU

Nibsy's
££ - £££ Dessert Cafe British
www.nibsys.comk
26 Cross St, Reading RG1 1SN

The Griffin
££ - £££ Bar British Pub
www.chefandbrewer.com
10-12 Church Rd, Caversham, Reading RG4 7AD

Cafe YOLK
££ - £££ Quick Bites Cafe British

www.cafeyolk.com
44 Erleigh Rd, Reading RG1 5NA

Salisbury

Tinga
££ - £££ Mexican Vegetarian Friendly Vegan Options

www.tingasalisbury.com
2-4 Salt Lane, Salisbury SP1 1DU

Bird and Carter Deli Cafe
££ - £££ Specialty Food Market Cafe British

https://birdandcarter.co.uk
Warminster Rd, Chilhampton Farm, Salisbury SP2 0AB

Greengages Cafe
££ - £££ Cafe British Vegetarian Friendly

www.greengagessalisbury.co.uk
31 Catherine St, Salisbury SP1 2DQ

Thai Orchid
££ - £££ Asian Thai Vegetarian Friendly

www.thaiorchid-salisbury.co.uk
58A Fisherton St, Salisbury SP2 7RB

Old Mill Restaurant
££ - £££ Bar British Pub

oldmillhotelsalisbury.co.uk
Town Path West Harnham, Harnham, Salisbury SP2 8EU

Southampton

Bell Tower Tea Rooms
££ - £££ Cafe British Vegetarian Friendly

www.salisburycathedral.org.uk
Cathedral Close, Salisbury, SP1 2EJ,

Kohinoor Of Kerala
££ - £££ Indian Asian Vegetarian Friendly

www.facebook.com/KohinoorOfKerala
2 The Broadway, Portswood Rd, Southampton SO17 2WE

5 Rivers Sports Bar
££ - £££ Indian Bar Pub

www.5rivers.pub
30 Bevois Valley Rd, Southampton SO14 0JR

Tewkesbury

Jelly Roll Cafe
££ - £££ Cafe British Vegetarian Friendly

17 Barton St, Tewkesbury GL20 5PP

Salerno
££ - £££ Italian European Vegetarian Friendly

salernoitalianrestaurant.co.uk
Tewkesbury 67 Church St, Tewkesbury GL20 5RX

The Nottingham Arms
£ British Contemporary Vegetarian Friendly   130 High St, Tewkesbury GL20 5JU

Abbey Tea Rooms   www.facebook.com/abbeytearoomstewkesbury
££ - £££ Cafe British Vegetarian Friendly   59 Church St, Tewkesbury GL20 5RZ

Winchcombe

Wesley House   wesleyhouse.co.uk
££ - £££ European British Vegetarian Friendly   High St, Winchcombe GL54 5LJ

Food Fanatics   www.food-fanatics.co.uk
££ - £££ Quick Bites Cafe British   12 North St, Winchcombe GL54 5LH

The Corner Cupboard   www.cornercupboardwinchcombe.co.uk
££ - £££ Bar British Pub   83 Gloucester St, Winchcombe GL54 5LX

5 North St   www.5northstreetrestaurant.co.uk
££££ European British Vegetarian Friendly   5 North St, Winchcombe GL54 5LH

The Lion Inn   www.thelionwinchcombe.co.uk
££ - £££ Bar European British   North St, Winchcombe GL54 5PS

Kyoto Kitchen   www.kyotokitchen.co.uk
££ - £££ Japanese Sushi Vegetarian Friendly   70 Parchment St, Winchester SO23 8AT

The Fox   the-fox.pub
££ - £££ Bar British Vegetarian Friendly   Peach Hill Lane, Winchester SO21 2PR

Winchester

Winchester Cathedral Refectory   www.winchester-cathedral.org.uk
££ - £££ Quick Bites Cafe British   Visitor's Centre, Inner Close, Winchester SO23 9LS

Gurkha's Inn   www.gurkhasinnwinchester.com
££ - £££ Indian Asian Nepali   17 City Rd, Winchester SO23 8SD

Chesil Rectory   https://www.chesilrectory.co.uk
££££ European British Vegetarian Friendly   1 Chesil St, Winchester SO23 0HU

The Porterhouse
££ - £££   Steakhouse British Gluten Free Options

www.porterhouserestaurant.co.uk
24 Jewry St, Winchester SO23 8SB

Forte Kitchen
££ - £££   British Vegetarian Friendly Vegan Options

fortekitchen.co.uk
78 Parchment St, Winchester SO23 8AT

Windsor

Windsor Grill
££ - £££   Steakhouse Seafood European

www.windsorgrill.co.uk
65 St. Leonards Rd, Windsor SL4 3BX

The Fox and Castle
££ - £££   Bar British Pub

www.thefoxandcastleoldwindsor.com
21 Burfield Rd, Old Windsor, Windsor SL4 2RB

Punto Italian Pizzeria & Restaurant
££ - £££   Italian Pizza Vegetarian Friendly

www.restaurantpunto.co.uk
3 Wheatsheaf Pde, Old Windsor, SL4 2QH

Golden Curry
££ - £££   Indian Asian Balti

www.goldencurryeton.co.uk
46 High St, Eton, Windsor SL4 6BL

Wokingham

Rossini
££ - £££   Italian Mediterranean Vegetarian

www.rossini-restaurant.com
16 Denmark St, Wokingham RG40 2BB

Ruchetta
££££   Italian European Vegetarian Friendly

www.ruchetta.com
6 Rose St, Wokingham RG40 1XU

Pãn
££ - £££   Asian Contemporary Fusion

www.panrestaurant.co.uk
47-49 Peach St, Wokingham RG40 1XJ

Piccolo Arco
££ - £££   Italian Sicilian Southern-Italian

www.piccoloarco.com
Unit 2-4 Town Hall, Wokingham RG40 1AS

The Tamarind Tree
££ - £££   Indian Asian Balti

www.the-tamarind-tree.co.uk
54 Peach St, Wokingham RG40 1XG

Chef Peking
££ - £££   Chinese Asian Cantonese

www.chefpeking.co.uk
426 Finchampstead Rd, Wokingham RG40 3RB

Xenuk Tandoori Restaurant
££ - £££   Indian Asian Bangladeshi

www.xenuk.co.uk
428 Finchampstead Rd, Finchampstead,
Wokingham RG40 3RB

The Green Man
££ - £££   Bar British Pub

www.greenmanhurst.co.uk
Hinton Rd, Hurst, Wokingham RG10 0BP

Yate

The Vintage Birdcage Cakery
££ - £££   Dessert Cafe British

www.vintagebirdcage.co.uk
Grooms House Stanshawes Ct,
Yate BS37 4DZ

CAMPSITES

Campsites all have their own distinct personalities–some are vast and sprawling with things like discos, children's play areas, cafes, shops and even swimming pools. Others have a much wilder, back-to-basics vibe, so be mindful of the kind of camping experience you want and make sure you choose your campsite accordingly. Once you've chosen a campsite, before you arrive, make sure you are aware of the campsite's rules. These can range from absolutely no noise after 9pm to no music, dogs or campfires, so make sure you are aware of the rules and that you stick to them. Make sure you know check in and check out times and print out some details, just in case your phone goes flat.

Berkshire

Scotlands House Campsite www.scotlandshouse.co.uk
Scotlands House, Forest Rd, Warfield, Bracknell RG42 6AJ

Gloucestershire

Winchcombe Camping & Caravanning Club campingandcaravanningclub.co.uk
Brooklands Farm, Tewkesbury GL20 8NX

Cotswold Farm Park cotswoldfarmpark.co.uk
Guiting Power, Cheltenham GL54 5FL

Tewkesbury Abbey Caravan and Motorhome Club Campsite caravanclub.co.uk
Gander Ln, Tewkesbury GL20 5PG

Croft Farm Water Park croftfarmwaterpark.com
Bredon's Hardwick, Tewkesbury GL20 7EE

Gloucester Camping at Court Farm. gloucestercampingatcourtfarm.com
Court Farm, Tewkesbury Rd, Gloucester GL2 9PX

Elmwicke Camping elmwicke.co.uk
Red House Farm Copse Green Lane, Cheltenham GL51 9TB

Lower Lode Inn lowerlodeinn.co.uk
Bishops Walk Nr Tewkesbury, Gloucester GL19 4RE

Briarfields Motel & Touring Caravan Park briarfields.net
B4063, Cheltenham GL51 0TS

Cheltenham Racecourse Caravan and Motorhome Club Site caravanclub.co.uk
Prestbury Park, Prestbury, Cheltenham GL50 4SH

Pelerine Caravan & Camping Site — newent.biz
34 Ford House Rd, Newent GL18 1LQ

Tudor Caravan Park — tudorcaravanpark.com
Shepherds Patch, Slimbridge, Gloucester GL2 7BP

Hogsdown Farm Caravan and Camping Site — hogsdownfarm.co.uk
Wick Rd, Dursley GL11 6DD

The Riverside Caravan Park at The George Inn
Bristol Rd, Cambridge, Gloucester GL2 7AL

Apple Tree Park Caravan and Camping Site — appletreepark.co.uk
A38, Claypits, Gloucester GL10 3AL

Morn Hill Caravan and Motorhome Club Campsite — caravanclub.co.uk
Alresford Rd, Winchester SO21 1HL

Folly Farm Caravan and Campsite Winchester — follyfarmcaravanpark.com
Crawley, Winchester SO21 2PH

Rivermead Campsite — rivermeadcs.com
1 Weston Colley, Micheldever, Winchester SO21 3AF

Three Trees Campsite — threetreescamping.co.uk
Ampfield hill, Romsey SO51 9BD

Rookesbury Park Caravan and Motorhome Club Campsite — caravanclub.co.uk
Hundred Acres Rd, Wickham, Fareham PO17 6JR

ScottsHaven Caravaning Touring Site — scottshaven.co.uk
May Bush Ln, Southampton SO32 3QF

Solent Breezes Holiday Park — parkholidays.com
Hook Ln, Warsash, Southampton SO31 9HG

Chichester Camp & Caravan Club Site — campingandcaravanningclub.co.uk
345 Main Rd, Southbourne, Emsworth PO10 8JH

Tom's Field Camping New Forest — tomsfield.com
The Ridge, Pottery Rd, Fordingbridge SP6 2LN

Hill Cottage Farm — hillcottagefarmcampingandcaravanpark.co.uk
Sandleheath Rd, Alderholt, Fordingbridge SP6 3EG

Jubilee Camping jubileecamping.co.uk
Browns Ln, Damerham, Fordingbridge SP6 3HD

Middlesex

Wyatts Covert Caravan and Motorhome Club Campsite caravanclub.co.uk
Tilehouse Ln, Denham, Uxbridge UB9 5DH

Oxfordshire

Swiss Farm Touring and Camping swissfarmcamping.co.uk
Marlow Rd, Henley-on-Thames RG9 2HY

Henley Four Oaks Caravan and Motorhome Club Campsite caravanclub.co.uk
Marlow Rd, Henley-on-Thames RG9 2HY

Bridge Villa Camping and Caravan Park bridgevilla.co.uk
The St, Crowmarsh Gifford, Wallingford OX10 8HB

Oxford Camp & Caravan Club Site campingandcaravanningclub.co.uk
426 Abingdon Rd, Oxford OX1 4XG

Burford Caravan and Motorhome Club Campsite caravanclub.co.uk
Bradwell Grove, Burford OX18 4JJ

Surrey

Chertsey Camp & Caravan Club Site campingandcaravanningclub.co.uk
65-67 Bridge Rd, Chertsey KT16 8JX

Laleham Camping Club www.lalehamcampingclub.co.uk
Thames Side, Staines-upon-Thames, Staines TW18 1SS

Walton on Thames Camp & Caravan Club campingandcaravanningclub.co.uk
Fieldcommon Ln, West Molesey, Molesey, Walton-on-Thames KT12 3QG

Wiltshire

Oakley Farm Caravan Park oakleyfarm.co.uk
Penwood Rd, Newbury RG20 0LR

Brook Lodge Farm Camping & Caravan Park brooklodgefarm.com
Brook Lodge Farm, Bristol BS40 5RB

Plough Lane Caravan Site — ploughlane.co.uk
Plough Lane Caravan Site, Kington Langley, Chippenham SN15 5PS

Piccadilly Caravan Park — piccadillylacock.co.uk
Folly Ln W, Lacock, Chippenham, SN15 2LP

Devizes Camping & Caravanning Club Site — campingandcaravanningclub.co.uk
Spout Ln, Melksham SN12 6RN

Blackland Lakes — blacklandlakes.co.uk
Stockley Ln, Calne SN11 0NQ

Burton Hill Caravan and Camping Park Ltd — burtonhill.co.uk
20 Burton Hill, Malmesbury SN16 0EH

Salisbury Camp & Caravan Club Site — campingandcaravanningclub.co.uk
Hudson's Field, Castle Rd, Salisbury SP1 3SA

Summerlands Caravan Park — summerlandscaravanpark.co.uk
Rockbourne Rd, Salisbury SP5 4LP

Salisbury Hillside Caravan and Motorhome Club Campsite — caravanclub.co.uk
Andover Road, Lopcombe Corner, Salisbury SP5 1BY

Salisbury Campsite at Bake Farm — salisburycampsite.co.uk
Bake Farm, Salisbury SP5 4JT

Brades Acre Camp Site — bradesacre.co.uk
Brades Arce Campsite, Tilshead, Salisbury SP3 4RX

Hillcrest Campsite — hillcrestcampsite.co.uk
Salisbury SP5 2QW

Coombe Caravan Park — coombecaravanpark.co.uk
Coombe Bissett, Salisbury SP2 8PN

FURTHER READING

There is an excellent book which covers the life of Anne Boleyn and the places she visited in more detail. The painstaking work done to piece together the original royal route has influenced the route presented in this book.

In the Footsteps of Anne Boleyn by Sarah Morris and Natalie Grueninger (ISBN: 978-1445639444) is well worth a read. There is a whole chapter dedicated to the 1535 progress, plus coverage of her life at Hever and her time in the French court.

For general books on Henry's wives, his court and Henry himself, here is a selection.

The Life and Death of Anne Boleyn by Eric Ives OBE (978-1405134637) is a biography focusing on Anne's life and legacy, establishing her as a significant figure in her own right. The book ponders was she an adulteress or a victim? It also examines the issues that led to Anne's demise. She is discussed as a patron of the arts, especially in relation to Hans Holbein. Evidence of Anne's spirituality and interest in period intellectual debates during the period is also reviewed.

Two books about Henry's reign written by Alison Weir, *Henry VIII: King and Court* (978-0099532422), and *The Six Wives of Henry VIII* (978-0099523628) also go into more depth.

Thomas Cromwell: The untold story of Henry VIII's most faithful servant (978-1444782882) by Tracy Borman looks at Henry's 'right-hand man'.

For some short reads, check out our sister series of books, Hooked on History, which have short biographies of Henry VIII and Thomas Cromwell.

INDEX

Route overview	4
How to use this guide	6
The 1535 progress route	7
Who was King Henry Viii?	8
Overview	8
The need for a son	9
Tudor royal progresses	10
Why go on a progress?	10
Who else went on the progress?	11
How was a route decided?	12
Daily life in Henry's England	14
The royal court	14
The wider population	15
Tudor advancement... and downfall...	17
How Anne Boleyn became queen	19
Anne's rise	19
Henry and Anne In 1535	22
Tudor travel	23
Road conditions	23
Navigating	25
Hunting with hawks	27
Getting started	27
Choosing your bird	27
Understanding your bird	28
Training, diet, and exercise	28
Organising the hunt	29
Windsor	30
Windsor Castle	31
Windsor attractions	31
Windsor Castle	31
Dorney Court	32
Fudge Kitchen	32
Eton College and Museums	32
The Long Walk	32
Windsor Great Park	33
Reading	34
Reading Abbey	35
Reading attractions	36
Reading Museum	36
The Oracle Shopping Centre	36
Museum of English Rural Life	37
Silchester Roman City Walls and Amphitheatre	37
TimeTrap Escape Rooms	37
Ewelme Palace	38
Ewelme Palace	39
Abingdon	41
Abingdon Abbey	42
King John's Palace Langley	44
Langley, Oxfordshire	45
Sudeley Castle	47
Sudeley And Winchcombe	48
Winchcombe attractions	50
Winchcombe	50
Hailes Abbey	50
Tewkesbury	51
Tewkesbury Abbey	52
Gloucester	53
Gloucester Abbey	54
Gloucester attractions	54
International Centre for Birds of Prey	54
Briery Hill Llamas	55
Nature in Art	55
Soldiers of Gloucestershire Museum	55
Jet Age Museum	55
Gloucestershire environs	56
Painswick	57
Prinknash, Brockworth, Miserden	57
Leonard Stanley	59
Leonard Stanley	60
Berkeley Castle	61
Berkeley Castle	62
Berkeley attractions	63
Dr Jenner's House, Museum and Garden	63
Thornbury	64
Thornbury Castle	65
Iron Acton	66
Acton Court	67
Little Sodbury	69
Little Sodbury Manor	70
Aerospace Bristol	71
Dyrham Park	71
Chippenham Museum	71
Bowood House and Gardens	71
Bromham	72
Bromham House	73
Burbage	74
Wolfhall	75
Thruxton	76
Thomas Lisle's House	77
Bromham attractions	77
Atwell-Wilson Motor Museum	77
Lacock Abbey	77
Wiltshire Museum	78
Wadworth Brewery	78
Cherhill White Horse and Monument	78
Caen Hill Locks	79
Wilton Windmill	79
Crofton Beam Engines	79
Hurstbourne Priors	80
Hurstbourne Priors Manor	81
Hurstbourne Priors attractions	81
Whitchurch Silk Mill	81
Bombay Sapphire Distillery	81
Highclere Castle	82
Winchester	83
Wolvesey Palace	84
The Great Hall	85
Winchester Cathedral	85
Jane Austen's House	85
Bishop's Waltham	86
Bishop's Waltham Palace	87
Southampton	88
Southampton Castle or Merchant House	89
Southampton attractions	89

Solent Sky Museum	89
Beaulieu National Motor Museum	90
Exbury Gardens and Steam Railway	90
Portchester	**91**
Portchester Castle	92
Portsmouth attractions	93
The Mary Rose	93
Salisbury	**94**
Church House, Crane Street	95
Sailsbury attractions	95
Old Sarum	95
Salisbury Cathedral	96
Clarendon Palace	**97**
Clarendon Park and Palace	98
Sherbourne St John	**99**
The Vyne	100
Old Basing	**101**
Basing House	102
Basingstoke attractions	103
Milestones Museum	103
Bramshill	**104**
Bramshill House	105
Wokingham attractions	105
Dinton Pastures Country Park	105
Easthamstead	**106**
Easthampstead Palace	107
The Arrests In May 1536	**108**
Things begin to unravel	109
Sun 30 Apr 1536	109
Mon 1 May 1536	110
5pm Tues 2 May 1536	111
2pm Tue 2 May 1536	112
Thu 4 May 1536	113
The ones that 'got away'	**114**
Fri 5 May 1536	114
Mon 8 May 1536	114
The trials begin	**117**
Fri 12 May 1536	117
The Trials Continue	**119**
Mon 15 May 1536	119
Examining the trials	**121**
The effect of the rumour mill	121
Ladies-in-waiting statements	121
Cromwell's role and motives	123
The supposed Catholic faction	124
Was there a hidden faction?	124
Henry's psychology	125
The executions begin	**126**
Wednesday 17 May 1536	126
Friday 19 May 1536	127
The remainder of the reign	**130**
Henry's third marriage, Jane Seymour	130
Cromwell's fall	130
Henry's fourth marriage, Anne of Cleves	131
Henry's fifth marriage, Catherine Howard	133
Henry's sixth marriage, Katherine Parr	134
Edward VI	135
Tudor food	**137**
Overview	137

Make a Tudor recipe	**139**
Frumenty	139
Packing list	**140**
Phone apps and websites	**144**
Apps	144
Key websites	145
Handy tips for microcamping	**146**
Quick tips	148
Road trip games	**150**
Spotting things	150
Word games	150
Places to eat	**151**
Campsites	**159**
Further reading	**163**
Index	**164**

165

LOOKING FOR MORE CAPERS?
SIGN UP FOR FREE ALERTS

WWW.MICROCAMPERCAPERS.COM/ALERTS

Get the inside track on when a new route is released.

Sign up for our free alerts.

WWW.MICROCAMPERCAPERS.COM/ALERTS

ANOTHER ROUTE TO EXPLORE

DRIVE THE FOSSE WAY

MICROCAMPER CAPERS

THE ANCIENT ROMAN ROAD FROM EXETER TO LINCOLN

COPYRIGHT

Title: Drive Henry VIII and Anne Boleyn's royal road trip: Follow in the footsteps of the 1535 royal progress of England

First published in the UK in 2021 by Microcamper Capers

ISBN: 9798484311965

Although the publisher has taken reasonable care in preparing this book, we make no warranty about the accuracy or completeness of its content and to the maximum extent permitted, disclaim any liability arising from its use.

Printed in Great Britain
by Amazon